THE FRENCH
REVOLUTION

QUESTIONS AND ANALYSIS IN HISTORY

Edited by Stephen J. Lee and Sean Lang

Other titles in this series:

Imperial Germany, 1871–1918
Stephen J. Lee

The Weimar Republic
Stephen J. Lee

Hitler and Nazi Germany
Stephen J. Lee

Parliamentary Reform, 1785–1928
Sean Lang

The Spanish Civil War
Andrew Forrest

The British Civil Wars and the Interregnum
Graham Seed

The Renaissance
Jocelyn Hunt

Tudor Government
T. A. Morris

The Cold War
Bradley Lightbody

Stalin and Russia
Stephen J. Lee

THE FRENCH REVOLUTION

JOCELYN HUNT

ROUTLEDGE
London and New York

First published 1998
by Routledge
11 New Fetter Lane, London EC4P 4EE

Simultaneously published in the USA and Canada
by Routledge
29 West 35th Street, New York, NY 10001

© 1998 Jocelyn Hunt

Typeset in Grotesque and Perpetua by
Keystroke, Jacaranda Lodge, Wolverhampton
Printed and bound in Great Britain by
Clays Ltd, St Ives plc

British Library Cataloguing in Publication Data
A catalogue record for this book is available from the British Library

Library of Congress Cataloging in Publication Data
Hunt, Jocelyn
 The French Revolution / Jocelyn Hunt.
  p. cm. – (Questions and analysis in history)
 Includes bibliographical references and index.
  1. France–History–Revolution, 1789–1799–Causes. 2. France–
Politics and government–1789–1815. 3. France–Social
conditions–18th century. I. Title. II. Series.
 DC148.H855   1998
 944.04–dc21   98–13539
                CIP

ISBN 0–415–17885–1

CONTENTS

SERIES PREFACE

Most History textbooks now aim to provide the student with interpretation, and many also cover the historiography of a topic. Some include a selection of sources.

So far, however, there have been few attempts to combine *all* the skills needed by the history student. Interpretation is usually found within an overall narrative framework and it is often difficult to separate out the two for essay purposes. Where sources are included, there is rarely much guidance as to how to answer the questions on them.

The Questions and Analysis series is therefore based on the belief that another approach should be added to those which already exist. It has two main aims.

The first is to separate narrative from interpretation so that the latter is no longer diluted by the former. Most chapters start with a background narrative section containing essential information. This material is then used in a section focusing on analysis through a specific question. The main purpose of this is to help to tighten up essay technique.

The second aim is to provide a comprehensive range of sources for each of the issues covered. The questions are of the type which appear on examination papers, and some have worked answers to demonstrate the techniques required.

The chapters may be approached in different ways. The background narratives can be read first to provide an overall perspective, followed by the analyses and then the sources. The alternative method is to work through all the components of each chapter before going on to the next.

ACKNOWLEDGEMENTS

The author and publishers would like to thank the following for permission to reproduce material:

Blackwell publishers for extracts from *The French Revolution* vol. 1 by J. M. Roberts (1966); Addison Wesley Longman Ltd for extracts from *The Longman Companion to the French Revolution* edited by Jones (1988); Edward Arnold for extracts from *The French Revolution 1785–1797* by Hardman (1981); Dorling Kindersley Ltd for a cartoon from *Chronicle of the French Revolution*; Macmillan Press Ltd for extracts from *The French Revolution: Documents and Debates* by Cowie (1988).

While every effort has been made to trace and acknowledge ownership of copyright material used in this volume, the publishers will be glad to make suitable arrangements with any copyright holders whom it has not been possible to contact.

1

WHY DID THE FRENCH REVOLUTION BEGIN?

BACKGROUND NARRATIVE

The French Revolution began in May 1789, with the meeting of the Estates General. Each group in French public life expected its own interests to be served by the meeting, and the fulfilling and frustration of those expectations mark the start of the Revolution. This Assembly, meeting 175 years after the last, was a measure of the desperation of the French government. From his accession in 1774, Louis XVI had faced a worsening financial situation, compounded by the money and troops sent to assist the Americans in war against Britain. France failed to gain the expected benefits: the liberated colonists continued to trade mainly with Britain, and were slow to repay the French loans. Turgot had warned that the first shot would drive France into bankruptcy, and he was proved right.

The appointment of Necker as Director of Finances in 1776 was a popular one, since he financed the war by borrowing, issuing five- and seven-year bonds at rates of 8 per cent or more. In 1781, however, the need to find new lenders led to his publication of the highly optimistic 'Compte Rendu au Roi'. By the time Calonne became Finance Minister in 1783, willing lenders were hard to find, so radical action was needed. His first schemes were designed to 'create wealth' and might today be called Keynesian: in the eighteenth century, they were merely extravagant. His other strategy was to reform the entire taxation system. The Parlement was most unlikely to register these reforms, but his idea that an Assembly of

Notables would be more tractable was mistaken. It raised objections to these reforms and tried to establish a constitutional role for itself. Calonne was replaced by Archbishop Brienne, himself a member of the Notables. He, too, failed to persuade the Notables, who demanded that the representatives of the whole nation should be consulted. The next months were spent in trying to persuade the Parlement to accept the reforms, while the financial situation worsened and public order was threatened. By August 1788 the King was forced to agree to the summoning of an Estates General for the next May, and to reappoint the ever-popular Necker. Decisions about the precise structure of the Estates General were assigned to a second Assembly of Notables, and rules for election were agreed. The Assembly which had seemed impossible in 1786 met at Versailles in May 1789.

The question of why the Revolution began has long been a matter of historiographical debate. One of the clearest discussions of the debate can be found in *Rethinking the French Revolution* by G. C. Comninel.[1] Marxist historians assert that this was a social revolution: a fundamental process of historical development. Barnave, in his *Introduction à la Révolution Française* (1792), had written that commercial property was totally different from and much more valuable than traditional landed property; thus the Revolution aimed to align political power with economic wealth. Barnave could be said to have predicted Marx. Later Marxist historians concurred. Lefebvre, for instance, wrote 'The Revolution is only the crown of a long economic and social evolution which has made the bourgeoisie the mistress of the world'.[2] And, for Marxists, the bourgeois revolution is the inevitable precursor of the proletariat revolution, since 'the bourgeoisie, wherever it has got the upper hand, has put an end to all feudal, patriarchal, idyllic relations' (*Communist Manifesto*).[3]

Historians who reject the determinist view prefer to argue that this was a revolution led by ideas: concepts like egalitarianism, justice, organisational rationalism and anticlericalism led to a search for a better society. R. R. Palmer, Jacques Godechot and Claude Manceron have put forward a conservative/liberal view that Revolution was needed to restore justice. They agree that a wider movement can be traced, linking the American and Dutch experiences to that of the French. J. M. Thompson provides a theoretical link between the Marxists and these historians, suggesting that the bourgeois and liberal nobles used their wealth in a creditable way to improve society. Among those who argue for a less clear cut view are Cobban and Doyle. Historians such as Souboul and Rudé add the dimension of the popular revolution, and the involvement of the *menu peuple*: the peasants in 1789, for example, and the *sansculottes*.

The two analyses in this section consider two aspects of these many arguments: Were the privileged classes responsible for the outbreak of the French Revolution? Is it possible to say that the Revolution was a middle-class phenomenon?

ANALYSIS (1): WERE THE PRIVILEGED CLASSES RESPONSIBLE FOR THE OUTBREAK OF THE FRENCH REVOLUTION?

The privileged classes could be held responsible in three ways: they helped cause the problems since their wealth was not subject to serious taxation; they provoked the hatred of the groups below them in society; and they used the strength of their position to resist attempts at change, while finally demanding, for their own ends, the meeting of the Estates General which gave voice to the Third Estate and ensured their own downfall.

Privilege was a complex concept in *ancien régime* France. The word lacked the modern connotation of injustice, since privilege was a form of property. The first two estates were identified as privileged. Manceron has this to say about the First Estate, the Church:

> The clergy is the first order of France, even richer in land and money than the nobility. The bishops, all of whom in the past century have come from the nobility, as well as the powerful abbots of the great monasteries, hold almost half the real estate of France. Property is presumed to be the product of accumulated centuries of endowments and is regarded as sacred, untouchable by any form of taxation. Every year, thanks to the tithe system . . . it grows'.[4]

Of course the Church did make its 'free gift' to the government every year, but it decided the amount itself, and was often in arrears.

The Second Estate, the nobility, for long had exemption from many taxes. *Capitation*, or tax per head, was paid by the nobility, but was divided into only four grades, and so did not hurt the rich. Nobles in the *pays d'état* paid the *taille*, but calculated their own contribution. The *vingtième* was the only proportional tax which the nobility paid. They resisted Calonne's planned single land tax precisely because it would have been collected according to size and value of holdings, regardless of the social status of the land holder.

Members of the nobility, and of the clergy, were also involved in capitalist enterprises. France was potentially a very rich country. As well as the range of climate and crops which should have ensured its wealth, it had a growing population, rich mineral resources, colonial possessions abroad and harbours on both the Mediterranean and Atlantic coasts. But the French government could not tap this wealth in taxation, since the tax systems dated from the Middle Ages, using land as the measure of wealth: even the *vingtième*, collected in peacetime since 1749, was assessed on 'real property'. Thus, either directly or indirectly, it was the common people who bore the weight of taxation; and not all of them: many towns had purchased exemption from *taille*. These *villes franches* did not pay the most oppressive taxes. Those who did were the *paysans* of France, the country folk. The King's government faced the thankless task of taking as much as it could from the very poor, while taking little from the wealthy. The failure of these sums to add up brought about the crisis which began the Revolution. Members of the prosperous classes collected certain taxes '*en ferme*': that is, they paid in advance for the right to collect the tax from a certain area. While this benefited the government, who got their money 'up front', it naturally meant that the taxpayer paid more, in order to cover their investment. And the system became less than adequate when the *fermiers généraux* took to 'paying' in IOUs rather than in actual money.

The *rentiers*, who invested in government stocks, were also, of course, the rich. They received their dividends and their repayments from those liable to tax, imposing a further burden on the poor.

The privileged classes also alienated the rest of society. The seigneurs, the land holders, whether clergy, noble, bourgeois or corporation, most directly oppressed the *paysans*. The peasants paid to the King the *tailles*, *vingtièmes*, *capitation* and the *gabelle* (salt tax); they also paid the *dîme* or tithe to the Church, but, above all, they paid their landlords. The luckiest, those who paid a fixed money rent, had actually benefited from the inflation of the 1770s. Others were *métayers*, share croppers, who gave between 40 per cent and 60 per cent of their produce to the landlord in return for the land and tools. In many areas, peasants still held their land according to the medieval rules of feudalism. They paid both in money and in kind for use of the land, and were liable to other obligations as well: the *banalités* of mill, oven, wine press and cider press were almost as hated as the hunting laws, which prevented them killing game animals, including pigeons and rabbits, building stone walls or harvesting crops till birds had finished nesting in them. There was little that peasants could do to resist their seigneurs: but, when events in Paris set the example, they liberated themselves in their own way, seizing the land and burning the infamous *terriers*, where their many obligations were set down. Many nobles had alienated their tenants still further, by employing *féodistes*, lawyers who specialised in discovering and enforcing forgotten feudal dues.

Some historians suggest that a further aspect of this 'feudal reaction' had been the attempt to close the ranks of the nobility to new entrants. In the past there had been various routes to attaining all the privileges of nobility: inheritance; purchase; direct grant from the King; or securing appointment to a position which carried with it nobility. 'Robe' nobles were resented by the nobles of the sword, although 'robe' nobles were accepted as 'sword' nobles after three generations, or 'four quarterings'. During the eighteenth century, formal decrees were made, limiting the officer ranks of the army and the senior jobs in Church and State to those with four quarterings. It may be that the wealthy bourgeoisie in their turn resented this closing of the doors to privilege and tax exemption.

Above all, it was the privileged classes who turned a financial crisis into a constitutional and political revolution. The Assembly of Notables refused to accept Calonne's reforms, or even Brienne's much less radical reworking of them. They, like the members of the Parlement, were reluctant to lose influence over future tax raising, and so refused to accept Calonne's permanent tax; the privileged classes attempted to retain some control over amounts, by demanding that his planned regional councils met '*par ordre*' and not simply according to size of land holding. When the Parlement rejected the decrees, and the King registered them by *lit de justice*, the *parlementaires* depicted themselves as protectors of the traditional rights of the French against the encroachment of the King, and, for a few months at least, convinced the people that they were defending liberty. When it became clear, in the autumn of 1788, that they were simply defending their own privileges, the reaction was all the stronger.

The arrogance of the privileged groups can be seen in their intention to use the Estates General for their own ends. If the meeting had been in the form of 1614, the three estates would have had equal numbers.

The domination of the privileged would have been further assured by meeting and voting '*par ordre*' so that there would always be a two to one majority against radical change. When Louis concluded that there should be double representation for the Tiers, the privileged hoped that this was to be the only change. The members of the Third Estate knew that the change in representation would be pointless without voting '*par tête*'. The refusal to meet separately was their first act of defiance.

Thus the privileged classes both prevented the Crown from solving its financial problems and escalated these problems into a full-scale revolution. On the other hand, the vocal and belligerent response of the prosperous and educated members of the Third Estate, and the pro-reform attitudes of some of the nobles are also significant factors. Nobles had resisted the king in every century of French history, without the far-reaching repercussions experienced in the 1780s and 1790s.

Questions

1. Would it have been possible for the Crown to reform the entrenched systems of French class and privilege without a revolution?
2. Does the fact that the privileged classes 'lost' in the French Revolution help to explain why they are blamed for bringing it about?

ANALYSIS (2): WAS THE REVOLUTION A 'MIDDLE CLASS' AFFAIR?

For the purposes of this section, a pragmatic approach has been taken to the term 'middle class'. It designates the people who were not the very poor, and who were not members of the two privileged orders. The term *bourgeoisie* is often used, but the implication of an urban class is not always appropriate. In the context of the late eighteenth century it is possible to identify a group of people who were educated, had income available for the purchase of books and papers, and had leisure to follow current affairs. While many of these would be from the commercial and professional classes, some would also be members of the wealthier peasantry. The educated classes played a major part in the actual summoning of the Assembly: in the period between November 1788 and the meeting of the Estates General, over 2,500 leaflets were published, including Dr Guillotin's 'Pétition des citoyens domiciliés à Paris', Marat's 'Offrande à la Patrie', and several by Desmoulins,

Brissot and Robespierre. The privileged classes also participated: Condorcet wrote seven pamphlets between November and February; Sieyès produced three during the same period. Their readership was predominantly in the salons and discussion clubs which the middle classes shared with the liberal nobles.

These groups were interested in the Enlightenment and its publications. Raymond Birn's essay[5] demonstrates that, by 1780, 40 per cent of servants and 30 per cent of salaried workers in Paris had one or more books according to their wills or death inventories. Amongst royal officials in the provinces, this rose to 74 per cent. Books which were banned in France were smuggled in from Switzerland and the Netherlands. The Philosophes of the Enlightenment were by no means in favour of equality for all. But they were vehemently anti-clerical (Voltaire and Holbach); they demanded the equalisation of justice (Condorcet and Diderot), fairer taxation (Quesnay) and the opportunity for all citizens to participate in government (Rousseau). These and other ideas had become part of the conversational currency of the educated classes by the 1780s, as never before. Discussion now focused on what was possible and desirable rather than what was traditional. The government had been influenced by Enlightenment ideas to some extent, not always usefully. The Eden Treaty of 1786, providing partial physiocratic free trade with Britain, did not help France's developing industries. It could be argued that the King's desire for reform were a measure of his interest in the new ways: certainly few kings before him had consulted as many groups as he and his ministers did in 1787–9. The publication of accounts by Necker, and subsequent demands for public scrutiny, also demonstrate the questioning mood of the Enlightenment.

Historians including Jacques Godechot and Claude Manceron have associated the French Revolution with similar developments in north Italy, in the Netherlands and in America, where the commercial classes tried to enhance their power at the expense of the traditional ruling classes. Events in America had a particular influence. The most obvious connection is that between Necker's borrowing (on five- to-seven-year terms starting in 1778–81) and the urgent need to sort out the French public debt in 1786–8. Historians such as Macdonald have argued that the influence on the educated classes of the war was even more important. He cites the Revolutionary mood in areas such as the Ile de France, which sent more troops to America than others. There may, of course, be other explanations for the uneven spread across France of Revolutionary fervour, and it is easy to point out prominent Revolutionaries who had never been farther from their homes in Arras

(Robespierre) and Champagne (Danton) than Paris. It can be said with some certainty, however, that the middle classes were interested in the American Revolution; they lionised the Marquis of Lafayette as someone with practical experience of liberty, and drew parallels between the tyranny of King George III and the ministerial despotism they perceived in their own country. Louis may well have regretted the freedom allowed to authors writing about the injustice of taxation without representation.

The impact of the educated classes was bound to be substantial once the system of government was questioned in any way at all. Decades of discussion and criticism by the Philosophes and their readers, together with close contact with the various British reform groups of the 1770s and 1780s, had introduced and made current the vocabulary and concepts necessary for constitutional and political change. The recalcitrance of the privileged classes provided the platform from which the middle classes could address their own agenda.

Questions

1. What 'Enlightenment' issues are discernible in the discussions which led up to the summoning of the Estates General?
2. Was the impact of the American war an essential catalyst to developments in France?

SOURCES

The first group of sources offers insights into the privileged classes and the part they played in events leading to the outbreak of the French Revolution. The second group looks at various perceptions and theories held at the time about the issues and events. In the Questions following the Sources, the number of marks that might be allocated by examiners is shown in square brackets.

1. THE PRIVILEGED CLASSES AND THE REVOLUTION

Source A: Controller-General Calonne speaks at the opening of the Assembly of Notables, 22 February 1787.

A general survey has led His Majesty to consider, first, the different forms of administration which exist in the different provinces of the kingdom where there is no meeting of the estates. To ensure that the levying of public taxes is no longer unequal and arbitrary in these areas, he has resolved to put the problem into the hands of the land owners themselves . . .

After considering inequalities and inadequacies in taxation, His Majesty has decided that the best method of remedying these inconveniences . . . would be to replace the *vingtièmes* by a general levy, which would apply to the whole realm . . . there would be no permitted exceptions, even including the royal domain, nor any variations other than those arising from the different qualities of soil and variety of crops. The property of the Church must necessarily be included in this general reorganisation . . .

Source B: the President of the Parlement's speech at the Lit de Justice, 6 August 1787.

Your Parlement, afflicted by the thought that it has, for twelve years, given its approval to the accumulated levies (and the suggested reforms would raise them to an increase of two hundred millions since Your Majesty's accession . . .) did not feel it had sufficient power to offer itself as a guarantee for the execution of these edicts before your people, who know no bounds to their love and their zeal, but who view aghast the mischievous conduct of an administration whose excessive depredations do not even appear to them to be possible . . .

Given the fact, Sire, that your Parlement finds it impossible to vote for such crushing taxes, it can only repeat its most eager reasons for supplicating Your Majesty . . . . that it will please you to agree to the summoning of the Estates General . . .

If, despite the supplications, arguments and representations of your Parlement, Your Majesty were still to feel obliged to make use of your absolute power, your Parlement would not cease to employ all its zeal and to raise its voice with as much firmness as respect, against impositions whose practice would be as disastrous as their concept is illegal . . .

Source C: extract from British Embassy despatches.

Hailes to Lord Carmarthen, 17 April 1788.
. . . The little success of the Minister who is at the head of the Finances, . . . owing chiefly to the persevering opposition of the Parlements, makes it believed that the Epoch of the Assembly of the States is near at hand . . .

Let it be even supposed (a thing scarcely possible) that the Nobility and Clergy should make a voluntary surrender of those privileges which make them . . . so much the objects of envy . . . ; there must still, should a constitution be attempted to be formed, remain a party to defend the Authority of the Sovereign, and another to attack and invade it. To draw the line between the prerogatives of the Prince and the Rights of the people is a work of such magnitude as could with difficulty be perfected by the most enlightened and disinterested Men, all concurring to the same end. To effect it with opposite and jarring interests is a task that appears next to impossible.

Source D: memorandum of the Princes of the Blood, 12 December 1788.

The writings which have appeared during this Assembly of Notables . . . all announce . . . an organised system of insubordination, and a distrust of the laws of the State. . . . Such is the unhappy progress of this effervescence, that opinions which some time ago would have seemed the most reprehensible seem today reasonable and just; and what men of property are indignant about nowadays will perhaps, in a little while, seem regular and legitimate. Who can say where the temerity of opinions will stop? The rights of the throne have been brought into question . . . ; soon the rights of property will be attacked; inequality of fortunes will be presented as a suitable subject for reform; already the suppression of the feudal dues has been suggested as if it were the abolition of a system of oppression, left over from barbarism.

It was made clear to Your Majesty how important it is to keep the single form of the convocation of the Estates General which is constitutionally correct . . . No one has tried to hide from Your Majesty the fact that to change the form of the summoning letters for the Third Estate alone and to call to the Estates General two deputies for this order, even if they are only given one vote as in the past, would be an indirect and oblique way of welcoming the pretensions of the Third Estate who . . . would not be inclined to be content with a concession which is pointless and without real interest, in that the number of deputies would be increased without the number of votes being changed.

(Artois, Condé, Conti, Bourbon, Enghien)

Source E: Council of State of the King, 27 December 1788.

The King having heard the report which was made in the council by the Minister of His finances . . . has ordered the following:

1. that the Deputies at the next Estates General shall be at least a thousand in number;
2. that the number shall be made up, as far as possible, according to the composition of both population and contributions of each *baillage*;
3. that the number of deputies in the Third Estate shall be equal to the number of the two other orders put together, and that this proportion shall be established by the letters of convocation.

Questions

*1. What was the Parlement? What is meant by the reference to the 'absolute power' of the King (Source B)? [3]
2. Compare the views given on royal authority in Sources A, D and E with the view expressed in B. [4]
3. Evaluate Source C as evidence about Brienne's plans and their probable success. [5]
4. Compare and contrast the points made in Sources C and D about the risks involved if the King should proceed with his reforms. To what extent are their predictions accurate? [5]
5. Using these sources and your own knowledge, discuss the stages by which the developments in France moved from fiscal issues to a potentially revolutionary crisis. [8]

Worked answer

*1. [This sort of question is designed to test knowledge of concepts. A brief but clear answer is all that is needed.]

The Parlement of Paris was the most influential of the thirteen senior law courts of France. As well as hearing important cases, and providing the career framework of the French legal profession, the Parlements registered the King's decrees, if they conformed with the natural law of France. Should the Parlement refuse registration, the King could, having heard their objections, enforce the registration at a ceremonial '*lit de justice*'.

2. IDEAS AND THEORIES ON THE EVE OF THE REVOLUTION

Source F: extracts from Arthur Young: *Travels in France.*

18 May. If the French have not husbandry to show us, they have roads. . . . and indeed for the whole way from Samer it is wonderfully formed; a vast causeway with hills cut to level vales; which would fill me with admiration, if I had known nothing of the abominable *corvées* that make me commiserate the oppressed farmers, from whose extorted labour this magnificence has been wrung.
31 May. The poor people, who cultivate the soil here, are *métayers*, that is, men who hire the land without ability to stock it; the proprietor is forced to provide cattle and seed, and he and his tenant divide the produce; a miserable system that perpetuates poverty and excludes instruction.

Source G: extract from L. S. Mercier: *Tableau de Paris* 1783–9.

The castles which bristle in our provinces and swallow up large estates possess misused rights of hunting, fishing and cutting wood; and these castles still conceal those haughty gentlemen . . . who add their own taxes to those of the monarch, and who oppress all too easily the poor despondent peasant. . . . The rest of the nobility surround the throne . . . to beg eternally for pensions and places. They want everything for themselves – dignities, employments and preferences; they will not allow the common people to have either promotion or reward, whatever their ability or their services to their country.

Source H: extract from British Embassy despatches.

Dorset to Lord Carmarthen 11th December 1788.
I must however observe . . . that the Provinces probably will not consider themselves as bound to follow any particular mode . . . for the election of Deputies to represent them at the Assembly of the Estates-General, unless it shall appear by the records to be conformable to the customs of former times on similar occasions; neither, it is thought, will the Tiers-Etat at any rate submit to a representation . . . judged by them inadequate to the magnitude of the proportion they hold in the State; for, by the calculation which has lately been made of the three Orders, it appears that the Clergy, not including the Religieux, amounted to 90,000 only; and that of the Nobility, even with all those who have purchased their titles, amounted to no more than 500,000: the disproportion therefore between the Tiers-Etat and the other two orders, taken together, is very considerable, the whole population of France being estimated at 24 millions . . .

M. Necker gains ground in the public opinion of which the gradual rise of the Funds is a sure proof.

Source I: extracts from the first part of *Qu'est-ce que le Tiers Etat*, January 1789.

The plan of this pamphlet is very simple. We have three questions to ask:
1st, What is the Third Estate ? Everything.
2nd, What has it been heretofore in the political order? Nothing.
3rd, What does it demand? To become something therein . . .

Chapter 1. The Third Estate is a complete nation
What are the essentials of national existence and prosperity? Private enterprise and public functions.

Private enterprise may be divided into four classes: 1st, since earth and water furnish the raw material for man's needs, the first class will comprise all families engaged in agricultural pursuits. 2nd. Between the original sale of materials and their consumption or use, further work . . . adds to these materials a second value

... perfecting the benefits of nature and ... increasing the gross produce ... in value. Such is the work of the second class. 3rd. Between production and consumption ... a group of intermediate agents ... comes into being; these are the dealers and merchants. ... 4th. In addition to these three classes ... a society needs many private undertakings which are directly useful or agreeable to the individual. This fourth class includes from the most distinguished scientific and liberal professions to the least esteemed domestic services. Such are the labours which sustain society. Who performs them? The Third Estate.

Public functions likewise ... may be classified under four well-known headings: the Sword, the Robe, the Church and the Administration. It is unnecessary to discuss them in detail in order to demonstrate that the third estate everywhere constitutes nineteen twentieths of them, except that it is burdened with all ... the tasks that the privileged order refuses to perform. Only the lucrative and honorary positions are held by members of the privileged order ...

Source J: letter from Gouverneur Morris to Carmichael, US Chargé d'affaires in Madrid, 25 February 1789.

... Fayette is out of town. He is gone to Auvergne to get himself elected, either for the Noblesse or the Tiers Etat. I hope the former, for he would otherwise, in my opinion, be too desperately estranged from those of his own Class ... I have here the strangest employment imaginable. A Republican, ... I preach incessantly respect for the Prince, attention to the Rights of the nobility, and moderation, not only in the object but in the pursuit of it. All this, you will say, is none of my business, but ... I love France and as I believe the King to be an honest and good man, I sincerely wish him well.

Questions

1. Explain the meanings of the terms 'corvée' and 'métayer' in Source F. On what grounds does Arthur Young disapprove of them? [3]
*2. What reservations would a historian have in relying on sources from British writers such as Source F and Source H? [4]
3. Assess the validity of the arguments in Source I about the status of the Third Estate. [5]
4. Compare the analyses of the Estates General elections offered in Source H and Source J. [5]
5. 'Problems which had existed for many decades were now being seen as unacceptable and in need of reform.' Use these sources and your own knowledge to confirm or refute this statement. [8]

Worked answer

*2. [This question tests a general understanding of the period as much as a comprehension of the sources.]

While the hostility of the American war had faded, there remained a British sense of superiority over the French. Arthur Young's account of his travels in France is full of criticism of French methods and attitudes, and his description of *métayage* is hardly couched in neutral terms. On the other hand, he travelled extensively in France and was, as far as agricultural practice is concerned, an expert. Dorset, like all Embassy officials, would be practised in information gathering; on the other hand, it is not clear where his statistical information comes from, or how much information he can gather from outside Paris. These men, as visitors in a foreign land, would have a limited understanding of what they were seeing; but their expertise makes their evidence useful.

2

WHEN DID DEVELOPMENTS IN FRANCE BECOME REVOLUTIONARY?

BACKGROUND NARRATIVE

The meeting of the Estates General on 5 May 1789 was a remarkable event, but not a revolutionary one, if revolutions are defined as violent developments, leading to radical changes in the structures of class, politics and power. During the next two months, the Third Estate established itself as the true representative of the people by the simple strategy of refusing to do as the King ordered: declaring that they could not verify their membership except as one Assembly, they held roll calls and expressed theatrical surprise that the first two estates were not present. Gradually, some of the clergy began to join them, and, on 17 June, they called themselves the National Assembly. The Oath of the Tennis Court, on 20 June, in direct defiance of the King and of the pretensions of the two privileged orders, confirms that, at Versailles, developments had certainly become revolutionary.

In Paris, meanwhile, regular meetings of voters at the Hôtel de Ville kept Parisians informed. Journalists met and argued at the Palais Royal. Versailles was barely twenty kilometres away, and news travelled easily. Thus, on 9 July, Parisians learned that the Assembly, defying the King's wishes, had taken the title of 'Constituent

Assembly'. The King's dismissal of Necker, on 11 July, was reported in Paris the next morning and was the signal for the *journées* which culminated at the Bastille. The consequences in Paris, with the establishment of the Commune and the *milice bourgeoise*, were matched by results at Versailles: the recall of Necker, and the King's acceptance of the Constitutional Committee.

Waves of violence throughout France, focusing particularly on the burning of the *terriers* and other documents, left the privileged classes little choice but to offer their Grand Gesture of 4 August, and a mood of optimism developed that changes could be made successfully.

Parisian suspicions that the 'court party' was planning some counter-revolutionary strike were, however, confirmed by the Flanders Regiment banquet on 1 October, with the tricolour cockade trodden underfoot, while officers affirmed loyalty to the King. Four days later, the 'March of the Women' brought the royal family to Paris. Once the Assembly was also in Paris, reforms proceeded rapidly and, apparently, calmly for almost two years.

The King's anxieties for his family, together with poor advice, and his personal anguish at the Church reforms, led to his desperate attempt to escape from France. The flight to Varennes ensured that he would not be trusted again; also, perhaps, that he would have no choice but to accept the Constitution. Meanwhile, riots at the 17 July pro-Republican demonstration which led to the Massacre of the Champ de Mars confirmed the end of the non-violent atmosphere of 1790 and early 1791.

A few days of violence in Paris had, on three occasions, turned the course of events. The question of who engineered the actions of the Paris mob, and how far the rest of France was involved, are frequently raised. The two analyses in this section consider these two issues.

ANALYSIS (1): WHO WAS RESPONSIBLE FOR THE VIOLENT DEVELOPMENTS IN PARIS?

No one was surprised when trouble broke out in Paris in July 1789, since rising bread prices, and an increased population had frequently in the past triggered unrest. Riots about economic issues were commonplace. In April, for instance, there had been trouble around the house of the wallpaper manufacturer Reveillon. He was accused of paying new workers less than the going rate. Violence ensued, and the crowd refused to disperse: they seized the opportunity of looting his food stores as well. But a political dimension also emerged, as the rioters shouted 'vive le Tiers Etat' amongst their other slogans. More ominous, for historians looking for undue political influence, was the fact that the mob was able to get at Reveillon's house because of the Duke of Orléans. He needed to get to the races at Charenton, and ordered the police barricades to be moved so he could get through. The mob rushed through the gap.[1] The twenty-five dead, magnified by rumour in Paris to as many as one thousand, may be seen as the first dead of the Revolution.

The Duke of Orléans was also instrumental in encouraging journalists. His Palais Royal was a meeting place for writers of the left, and Assembly men. Reporters who had been to Versailles would share information with their colleagues at the Palais. The 'menu peuple' of Paris had access to a remarkable number of newspapers and pamphlets. The number of newspapers increased from four in 1788 to 184 in 1789 and 335 by the end of 1790.[2] While not everyone could read, taverns and reading rooms provided copies, and news was passed from those who could read to those who could not. (In the 1890s, the historian Allain, using the measure of who could sign their names in the marriage register, concluded that about half of the men and a quarter of the women in France were literate,[3] though the ability to write one's own name is hardly proof of the ability to understand Marat, Desmoulins or any other political journalist.) Interest in Paris was also fed by a continuing stream of pamphlets (3,305 in 1789, 3,121 in 1790).[4] It seems reasonable to assume that the literate classes were influencing the ordinary people.

Many Parisians attended the meetings at the Hôtel de Ville and, after the March of the Women, the meetings of the Constituent Assembly in the Manège. Assembly proceedings were further debated at meetings in the districts of Paris, some of which summoned their Assembly men to report on debates and to be given voting instructions. The Cordeliers district, in particular, was a centre for political activists, local residents including Danton, Desmoulins, Marat and Fabre d'Eglantine; several newspapers were also published in the district. In its cafés, plans were made which would affect all of Paris. For example, in April 1791, when the King was prevented from attending Easter Mass at Saint-Cloud, it was a Cordelier battalion of the National Guard which unharnessed the horses.

Once the Assembly moved to Paris, the Breton Club established itself at the former convent of the Jacobins, and became the most influential of the political clubs. After the local government reforms, the Cordeliers Club was also set up. While not everyone could afford the membership fees of these clubs, the public were allowed to observe their debates, which provided a further source of information and inspiration. Plans for the Republican Festival on the Champ de Mars were made at the Cordeliers Club in the summer of 1791.

The people who were later to claim to, and receive, pensions as *vainqueurs de la Bastille* were not the very poor; many of them were small shopkeepers, clerks or property owners: they could be expected to make their own decisions about something as extraordinary as an armed assault on a major government building.

The Duke of Orléans was seen by many as the leader of the opposition, in much the same way as the Prince of Wales was emerging as the focus of hostility to George III. He had stirred up the scandal surrounding the Necklace Affair, was a Grand Master of Freemasonry and had been closely involved in the resistance of the Notables to royal reform suggestions. A member of the Second Estate, he joined the National Assembly on 25 June. As already mentioned, his Palais Royal was a centre for pamphleteers and journalists. He almost certainly lent – which was the same thing as giving – money to Danton and to others of the Cordeliers group. But did he do more than merely encourage writers and demagogues? And what was he hoping to achieve from all this?

His part in the Reveillon riots may well be coincidental; his involvement in the quiet rebellion of the Third Estate was deliberate. He was not the first to move, but he was one of the early 'converts' from among the Noblesse. Events on the eve of the Bastille point more closely to him. The customs posts around Paris were farmed out to various wealthy men. The conviction that it was these posts which were putting up the price of bread made them a target on 12 July, but those farmed by Orléans were not destroyed. When, on 12 July, Desmoulins led a mob from the Palais Royal, they carried wax busts of the Duke, as well as Necker, both draped in black, to signify the end of liberty.

The King, who had never liked his cousin, was inclined to believe that Orléans had been involved with the March of the Women, and refused to receive him at court the following year. Orléans appears to have been unable to decide which was his safest route to power: in September 1789, he was known to be having meetings with Mirabeau, but no concrete alliance resulted. His popularity withstood this contact: when in October he went on a quasi-diplomatic mission to England, the mob, convinced that he was being exiled, refused to allow him to leave for four days.

It seems clear that Orléans pictured himself as ruler of France, perhaps as regent for the young Dauphin, following the abdication of Louis XVI. Indeed, following the flight to Varennes and the suspension of the King, he was addressed as 'the First Frenchman' in the Jacobin Club and (in the absence of the King's brothers), was next in line after the Dauphin. However, on 26 June 1792, he formally declared that he would not be Regent of France. His supporters dressed this up as anything from loyalty to pure Republicanism, but it could be seen as a loss of nerve. He had not dominated the Assembly; he had not become as popular as his Cordelier friends; it was the clubs and the districts which were influencing the people, and not he. Not until September 1792 did the Commune, at his request, choose a new name for him – Philippe Egalité: and there were too many equals with a greater following than his. Six months after his name change he was arrested, and, seven months after that, was guillotined. All his high hopes, assuming that he had high hopes, had come to nothing.

The failure of Orléans's ambitions can be demonstrated more clearly than his involvement in, or responsibility for, the revolutionary events in Paris. What can be reasonably concluded, however, is that the mob in Paris was steered by a variety of influences. Demonstrations about the price of bread were converted into political rallies; key information, such as the sacking of Necker, was disseminated in a way which heightened its impact and encouraged mob action; journalists such as Desmoulins spoke at critical moments and with simple messages: a symbol as potent as the Bastille could be used as shorthand to indicate tyranny and the need for the people to make a stand. It is also important to remember that Paris was not a huge and sprawling city: a meeting at the Palais Royal could easily move across the road to the Tuileries Gardens and the Manège. A mob moving from the Hôtel de Ville to the Bastille might well release prisoners from La Force on the way. Thus it would be inaccurate to dismiss the people of Paris as mindless dupes of a few demagogues. On the other hand, there appears to be no question that they were fed information, and given suggestions as to how they might react to news, by educated men with a distinct agenda of their own.

Questions

1. Did events in Paris develop logically from each other, or is it more accurate to see them as a series of random expressions of popular feeling?

2. What are the problems which confront historians who attempt to apportion individual responsibility for mass movements and developments?

ANALYSIS (2): TO WHAT EXTENT DID PARIS DOMINATE THE EARLY STAGES OF THE FRENCH REVOLUTION?

The history of the Revolution is often described in terms of Paris, but this was certainly not the case at first. The country people of France had much to complain about and correspondingly high hopes of the Assembly when it met. The most radical *cahiers* were not those of Paris and, while some of them were written in a very humble style, several express their wishes much more as demands. While some made Parisian demands, such as the closure of the Bastille, many others had local concerns at their heart.

The dominant speakers of the Estates General were not Parisians, but came from provincial areas such as Artois (Robespierre) or the Auvergne (Lafayette) and the centre of left-wing ideas was the Breton Club. On the other hand, the nearness of Paris, and its large population, meant that it was bound to have an influence on events in Versailles, an influence obviously much increased once the royal family had moved to Paris. Mirabeau was one of several advisers who recommended that the King should move to a smaller and less volatile city, such as Rouen or Orléans.

News of events in Versailles and Paris was avidly read and discussed by people in the provinces. Some of the Paris newspapers were sent to other big towns; one, *La Feuille Villageoise*, was specifically aimed at country folk and, by 1791, had fifteen thousand subscribers, with, according to the usual estimates, a readership of four or five times that. Arthur Young complained how difficult it was to find newspapers, but after 20 July, when he heard the news of the Bastille in Strasbourg, he frequently met peasants wearing the cockade and had to explain on more than one occasion that he was not a 'seigneur'.

D. M. G. Sutherland[5] clearly demonstrates how much unrest and violence there was in the countryside, even before the *Grande Peur* of July 1789 (for example, the insurrections in Flanders, and around Mâcon). But news of the fall of the Bastille did mark a new stage in widespread and serious riots, attacks focusing on the mechanisms of feudalism and rural oppression. Without the *Grande Peur*, the nobles of the Constituent Assembly would not have been forced into their grand gesture.

From October 1789 onwards, Paris dominated events; but other parts of France also had roles to play. Had it not been for Drouet, the postmaster of Sainte-Menehould, and the townspeople of Varennes, the King and his family might have reached the frontier in June 1791. Fraternal Jacobin Clubs, and federated *milice bourgeoise* groups were established in most towns, reporting to their parent bodies in Paris only when it suited them. During 1792, it was the *fédérés* who decisively turned events at the Tuileries.

On the other hand, the countryfolk who formed the vast mass of the French population do seem to have felt that events were passing beyond their grasp.[6] Once they had seized the demesne lands, killed the game animals and burned the *terriers* which recorded their feudal obligations, they took little part in the Revolution. In many areas, villagers were shocked at the religious changes, concerned for the safety of their souls once the politicians in Paris had removed the Holy Father. Counter-Revolution was a provincial rather than a Parisian phenomenon. Those in Paris who disliked the work of the Constituent Assembly, or who were frightened by the violence, tended to leave and move into the countryside. The more affluent, of course, left the country altogether, and at first there was little attempt to stop them, perhaps on the basis that, abroad, they would be less of a threat. Some of the best known writers of the counter revolution, such as Rivarol and D'Antraigues, emigrated early, and carried on their propaganda war from abroad. Groups and areas which objected to the religious reforms, and to the treatment of the King, did little in the first few years of the revolution, although the Breton Association's plans for an armed landing in 1792 were endorsed by the Count of Artois. It was to be the levy of February 1793 which would rouse the Vendée and Brittany into full-scale counter-revolution. The counter revolution may be seen as a response in the provinces to the domination established by Paris over the affairs of France.

The Revolutionary movement had developed in France as a whole, and was led by people from all parts of France. The grievances it addressed at the start were felt by the whole population. Within a few months, however, Paris began to dominate. In some instances, the provinces can be seen as imitating, or at least following the lead of Paris. But there were strong feelings, both for and against the changes, all over France. The people who brought the King back from Varennes, or who attempted to stop Orléans leaving Boulogne, were not Parisians. And criticism of the revolutionary changes was to be heard expressed far more vigorously outside Paris than within it.

Questions

1. What were the physical problems which limited close links between Paris and the rest of France?
2. How far is it possible to say that the demands of the mass of the people of France had been met by the end of 1789?

SOURCES

The first group of sources considers events in Paris and Versailles, and the various interpretations which have been placed on them. The second group looks at how far the rest of France was concerned in these events.

1. EVENTS IN PARIS AND VERSAILLES

Source A: extract from the Diary of Gouverneur Morris.

20 June 1789.
This morning the different Corps of the Estates General were prevented from meeting ... The reason assigned is that the King intends to have a Séance Royale on Monday and that some alterations are necessary to the Salle.

Source B: 20 June letter from Necker to the Lieutenant of the Paris police.

The Chamber of the States General having been closed through absolute necessity, and the Deputies of the Tiers having met in another place, the public might believe that the intention of the King is to dissolve the Estates General; it is essential, Lieutenant, that you should make it understood in all Paris, that the King is, as always, concerned in re-establishing union and harmony for the happiness of his people, and that the sessions of the Estates General will recommence next Monday.

Source C: Lavaux, a lawyer, writing much later, about a visit to the Cordelier district on 13 July.

I saw my colleague, Danton, whom I had always known as a man of sound judgement, gentle character, modest and silent. What was my surprise at seeing him up on a table, declaiming wildly, calling the citizens to arms to repel fifteen thousand brigands gathered at Montmartre, and an army of thirty thousand poised to sack Paris and slaughter its inhabitants ... I went up to him and asked what all the uproar was about; I spoke to him of the calm and security I had seen at Versailles. He replied that . . . the sovereign people had risen against despotism. 'Join us', he said. 'The throne is overturned and your old position is lost. Don't forget that.'

Source D: from 'Les Révolutions de Paris', no. 1, 17 July 1789.

Meanwhile the attackers marched out amidst an enormous crowd: . . . cries of vengeance and delight sounded on all sides; the victors, triumphant and laden with honours, bearing the arms and trophies of the vanquished, the banners of victory, the militia mingling the soldiers of the fatherland, the tributes offered them on every side, all this formed a terrible and a splendid spectacle. When they reached the Place de Grève, the populace, impatient for revenge, did not allow de Launey nor the other officers to face the city's tribunal; wresting them from the hands of their captors, it crushed them underfoot one after the other; de Launey was stabbed a thousand times; his head was cut off and carried, streaming with blood, on the end of a spear . . . The events of this glorious day will astonish our enemies and foretell at last the triumph of justice and liberty.

Source E: Camille Desmoulins: *Discours de la lanterne aux Parisiens*, September 1789.

It is from the Palais Royal that the loyal citizens set out to snatch from the Abbaye prison the French Guards who had been detained . . . It is from the Palais Royal that the orders were issued to close down the theatres and go into mourning on 12 July. It is at the Palais Royal that . . . the call to arms was made and the national cockade adopted. It is the Palais Royal which for six months has inundated France with all the brochures that have made of everyone, even the soldier, a philosopher. It is at the Palais Royal that the patriots, mingling joyously with the cavalry men, the dragoons, the horse guards, the Swiss guards and the cannoneers , , , won over the whole army . . . It is the Palais Royal that saved the National Assembly and the ungrateful Parisians from a general massacre.

Source F: *The Times* 12 October 1789.

In the present instance, M. de la Fayette betrayed a pusillanimity of character unworthy of his high rank and military capacity. He was conscious that the orders he received were treacherous and unjust . . . but the threat of the mob struck such terror into him, that he chose rather to obey their commands, and bring his King in ignominy to Paris . . . In the evening, therefore, M. de la Fayette set out for Versailles, at the head of twenty thousand of the Parisian guard . . . He had been preceded in the morning by about eight thousand persons, chiefly

Fishwomen. . . . At two o'clock on Tuesday morning, a considerable number of the persons who were habited in women's dresses, but, as it since appears, were many of them guards . . . forced their way into the Palace, and up the staircases leading to the Queen's apartment, with an intent to seize and murder her.

Questions

1. Who was de Launey (Source D)? What was the 'national cockade' (Source E)? [2]
2. 'His high rank and military capacity' (Source F). To what is the writer referring? How far does *The Times*'s account agree with other accounts of these events? [4]
*3. What stylistic techniques does Desmoulins use (Source E) to emphasise the points he is making? Does the fact that he was a journalist affect the value of this source to a historian? [5]
4. Evaluate the reliability and usefulness of *each* of these sources as evidence for events in Paris in 1789. [6]
5. Use your own knowledge to assess the extent to which these sources provide evidence to indicate that events in Paris were *either* spontaneous *or* orchestrated by any individual or group. [8]

Worked answer

*3. [Questions on style need to be answered with direct reference to the actual words of the source: since the style is journalistic, there is a clear link between the two parts of the questions.]

The repetition of the words 'Palais Royal' is the most obvious technique used by Desmoulins to emphasise its importance to the Revolution. His account describes every significant event as having derived its impetus from the Palais Royal. He uses key words which were increasing becoming associated with the revolution – 'citizens' who are, of course, 'loyal'; the 'national cockade; he uses other emotive terms, such as 'joyously' and 'ungrateful'. Above all, he exaggerates for effect, claiming that 'everyone' has become a philosopher, that they have won over 'the whole' army; that what was averted was 'a general massacre'.

These are all journalistic techniques, and Desmoulins was of course a journalist. His evidence may be tainted because he was one of the regular 'members' of the Palais Royal group with a distinct axe to grind. On the other hand, he was a central figure at the Palais Royal, and was at the heart of revolutionary developments, a friend of some of the key leaders of the left, a former school mate of Robespierre's. It is reasonable for a historian to accept his inside knowledge, as well as making allowance for his obvious bias and his somewhat lurid style.

2. THE REVOLUTION OUTSIDE PARIS

Source G: preliminary *cahier* of the parish of Boisse.

... The Third Estate desires that instead of all the taxes which it is forced to pay, they should be reduced to one, which the Third Estate desires shall be paid equally by lords, Churchmen and the Third Estate according to the possessions of each.... They beg also that the King should regard his people with pity and liberate them from this miserable scourge of the *gabelle* which, by its name alone, makes the universe tremble ... The Third Estate also beg His Majesty to lift from us the *banalité* of ovens and mills; in doing this, Sire, you would liberate your people from a great scourge, because it does happen that, thanks to the *banalité*, a miller can rob a subject, and he dares not object ...

Preliminary cahier of the parish of Longues
We, representatives of the parish of Longues, by the order which the King sent us, have called together the general assembly of all the inhabitants of the parish this 8 March, to list their grievances ...

1. We beg His Majesty to abolish all *gabelles*, and that salt shall become freely marketable ...
7. We beg His Majesty to give us the power to destroy the game which has multiplied too much and causes considerable loss in the countryside, namely rabbits and pigeons ...

Source H: Arthur Young at Strasbourg, 20 July 1789.

On arriving at the inn hear the interesting news of the revolt in Paris. The Gardes Français joining the people; the little dependence on the rest of the troops; the taking of the Bastille; and the institution of the *milice bourgeoise*; in a word, the absolute overthrow of the old government. Everything being now ... in the hands of the Assembly, they have the power to make a new constitution, such as they think proper; and it will be a great spectacle for the world to view, in this enlightened age, the representatives of twenty-five millions of people sitting on the construction of a new and better order and fabric of liberty than Europe has yet offered. ... I hear nothing of their removing from Versailles; If they stay there under the control of an armed mob, they must make a government that will please the mob; but they will, I suppose, be wise enough to move to some central town, Tours, Blois or Orléans, where their deliberations may be free. But

---

the Parisian spirit of commotion spreads quickly.... They have a cry among them that will conduct them to good lengths: – *point d'impôt et vivent les états.*

Source I: a complaint to the National Assembly by the Comte de Germiny, 20 August 1789.

On 20 July 1789, a gang of foreign brigands, joined with my vassals and those of the neighbouring parish... came to my Château of Sassy, ... in a crowd of about two hundred and, having broken the locks in the chests which contain my title deeds, they took a large number of them, with registers which are necessary to me and carried them off and burned them in the woods near my chateau; my guard could make no resistance, because he was the only guardian in this area, since I do not reside here. These wicked men rang the church bells in neighbouring parishes to gather even bigger numbers together... Who can ever assess and prove the damage which they have done to my properties? I call upon your good judgement, that these difficulties may be adjusted by the National Assembly, to restore to me what I have lost, and above all to provide me with some legal standing: necessary to my parishioners and my property, since the titles have been burned. I shall take no legal action against those whom I knew amongst these brigands who, not content with burning my papers, have killed all my pigeons.

Source J: Antoine, Comte de Rivarol, writing in *Le Journal Politique National*, 1790.

Paris has never merited the name of capital more than today: it raised the standard and the whole kingdom fell in behind it; it took for itself the name '*patrie*'.... and this insolent sophism has aroused no one's indignation. Paris absorbs all the State's revenue, it holds in its hands all the branches of authority, its Palais Royal draws up the proscription lists, its population carries them out... Three million armed peasants, from one end of the kingdom to the other, stop travellers, check their papers, and bring the victims back to Paris; the town hall cannot protect them from the fury of the patriotic hangmen; the National Assembly in raising Paris might well have been able to topple the throne, but it cannot save a single citizen. The time will come... when the National Assembly will say to the citizen army, 'You have saved me from authority, but who will save me from you?' When authority has been overthrown, its power passes inevitably to the lowest classes of society.... Such is today the state of France and its capital.

Source K: account by Drouet, postmaster at Sainte-Menehould, a few miles from Varennes.

It was eleven at night ... everyone in Varennes was in bed; the carriages were drawn up alongside the house and there was a dispute going on ...; the postmaster at Clermont had forbidden the postillions to continue beyond Varennes without first refreshing their horses. The King, fearing that he might be pursued, was trying to hasten their departure and would not hear of any time for refreshment; so that while they were disputing we ran quickly into the town and left our horses at an inn which we found open. I spoke to the Innkeeper; I took him aside, because ... I did not want to be overheard. I said: 'Are you a good patriot?' 'Yes, you may depend upon it,' came the answer. 'Good, my friend, run quickly and alert all whom you know to be honest men, tell them that the King is at the top of the town, and that ... we must stop him.'

Questions

1. Explain the meaning of the terms '*gabelle*,' '*banalité*' (in Source G) and '*milice bourgeoise*' (in Source H). [3]
2. Comment on the use of the words 'foreign brigands' (in Source I) and 'patriot' (in Source K). What does the use of these phrases tell you about the attitudes of the people who used them? [4]
3. What can be learned from Sources G, H and I about the attitudes of country people in France towards the Revolution? [5]
*4. Discuss Arthur Young's perceptions of events in Paris and Versailles. How accurate are his predictions of future developments? [5]
5. Using your own knowledge and the information contained in these sources, consider the extent to which developments in the provinces occurred independently from the developments in Paris. [8]

Worked answer

*4. [Part of this question requires textual analysis with commentary; it is also an opportunity to show that you understand the terms Young uses; the second part requires you to make use of your own knowledge. You need to make sure that you deal with both parts of the question.]

Writing at a distance, both of time and place, Young is right about the main events: the Bastille, the establishment of the National Guard and the right of the Assembly to make a Constitution. On the other hand, he exaggerates the immediate effects: the rest of the troops in fact remained loyal; the old government was not absolutely overthrown at this stage, nor was the kingdom in the hands of the Assembly, although these were to be the developments of the next few years. He recognises the risks of being close to Paris, and assumes, as Mirabeau recommended, that the Assembly will move to some other town in France. There is an element of cynicism in his 'great spectacle' comment, and yet he is right to comment that this is the first time that representatives of all the inhabitants of a country have been involved in constitutional discussion. Young recognises that a slogan of 'no taxes' is likely to be very popular, even if impractical.

As for making 'a government that will please the mob', Young could not, of course, predict that the finished Constitution would put power firmly in the hands of the middle classes; and that, while there were periods when the 'armed mob' influenced events and occasional policies, these were shortlived, and the urban poor in France benefited very little from the Revolution.

3

THE CONSTITUENT ASSEMBLY

BACKGROUND NARRATIVE

Although the status of laws passed by the Constituent Assembly (1789–91) was not entirely clear, since the King was often reluctant to sign them, they were nevertheless accepted as binding by the people of France as soon as they were agreed by the Assembly. First steps towards a constitution were taken in September 1789, when the King lost the right to prorogue or dismiss future assemblies; the King's veto was declared to be suspensive rather than absolute, and, from October, his title was to be 'King of the French' not 'of France'. He was not stripped of all his powers, however. Partly thanks to the arguments of Mirabeau, the King's right to declare war was confirmed in March 1790.

The Enlightenment principle of Separation of Powers was established with the decision of 7 November 1789, that royal ministers could not sit in the Assembly. The voting regulations of December introduced the distinction between active and passive citizens, and the local government reforms of the same month were intended to replace history and tradition with enlightened efficiency. It was also hoped that the abolition of the districts of Paris would curtail the revolutionary fervour of areas such as the Cordeliers.

Autumn 1789 marked the start of the judicial reforms, with the abolition of torture and 'permanent vacation' for the Parlements. Debates on equality of punishment were of particular interest to the well-read amateur philosophers of the Assembly, and consumed a great deal of time. The abolition of the manorial jurisdictions in February 1790 provided the vacant space on which the new judicial system could be built.

Enlightenment pressures within the Assembly ensured that the Church would not be ignored. In February 1790 the monastic orders were suppressed, and in May the sale of the Church lands began. The major institutional reforms were completed and accepted by the Assembly on 12 July, in the Civil Constitution of the Clergy, and the oath accepting it was imposed from November onwards, although the King did not sign the law until December.

Following the abolition of social distinctions in the August Decrees of 1789, the army reforms of February 1790 were essential: the ending of purchased commissions, and the principle of promotion by merit. This was not, however, the beginnings of an 'equal opportunities' regime. Attempts to liberate black slaves in the West Indies in May 1791 failed, not least because of the large numbers of slave owners (such as the de Lameths) in the Assembly. Nor did French workers fare better, since the Loi le Chapelier (June 1791) made *coalitions ouvrières* illegal.

Meanwhile, discussion of finance, the original reason for summoning the Estates General, had been deferred. *Assignats* had been issued for the first time in December 1789 and national ownership of the church's vast land holdings convinced some people that there would be enough money for everything: however, new and fair taxes were essential and, in November 1790, the *contribution foncière* (a single land tax) was announced. This was soon agreed to be insufficient, and in January 1791 the *contribution personnelle et mobilière* was added. In March the *patente* was decreed, the Assembly claiming that this payment could be made in place of subscriptions to the recently abolished guilds.

During the summer of 1791, additional touches were put to the Constitution; a decree in May prevented members of the existing Assembly from standing for election to the new Legislative Assembly. The soldiers' oath to the nation and its laws, agreed on 13 June, confirmed the change of focus away from the King. The Constitution was passed on 3 September and accepted by the King on 14 September. The new Legislative Assembly met on 1 October.

Discussion of the work of the Constituent Assembly tends to focus on the effectiveness of the legislation, both as compared to the needs of France at the time and in terms of the enduring quality of the institutions and ideals established. Was the Constitution of September 1791 a workable one: did it address the problems which confronted France? Once the structures were established, was there any likelihood that the monarchy in France could or would endure? The two analyses which follow consider these two aspects.

ANALYSIS (1): HOW TRUE IS IT THAT 'THE WORK OF THE CONSTITUENT ASSEMBLY BORE NO RELATIONSHIP TO THE REAL NEEDS OF THE FRENCH PEOPLE'?

The needs of the French people had, to an extent, been stated in the *cahiers*. But these documents were by their nature generalisations from all the preliminary *cahiers* which came from every village, guild and town council in each area; and the putting together of the documents had – unavoidably – been done by educated men. In Arras, for example, the guild of *sabot* makers, some of the poorest workers in the town, had asked the young lawyer Robespierre to write their *cahier* for them. Thus the *cahiers* which were presented in 1789 were not direct expressions of the needs of the masses. These needs were predominantly economic: the high levels of taxation and feudal obligation made even more acute the problems of peasants farming in old-fashioned and inefficient ways; in the towns, restrictive practices and heavy tolls reduced opportunities for enterprise; professions were restricted by all kinds of venality and by the expense of acquiring an education; the Church's wealth was concentrated at the top, with many of the lower clergy being scarcely able to support themselves, let alone provide welfare for their poorer parishioners.

When the Estates General met, however, its focus was on administrative and constitutional change, and on the judicial and religious systems of the country. There are various reasons for this. Several of the members, among them Mirabeau, noted that it was important to defer dealing with financial issues, lest the King seized the opportunity to close the Assembly down. In addition, many of the deputies were lawyers, or at least had had a legal training, and were more concerned with administrative structures than with the lifestyle of country people. Many of them, too, were educated in the ideas of the Enlightenment, and regarded the Separation of Powers and the Social Contract as being even more essential than the single land tax. Above all, France had been waiting for decades for the opportunity to consider its constitutional structure. The wide publicity given to events in America in the 1770s and 1780s meant that constitutional issues were discussed in salons all over France. As the members of those salons assembled at Versailles in their new roles as representatives, the same pre-occupations informed their new debates.

The principles for legislation were laid out in the August Decrees and the Declaration of the Rights of Man and of the Citizen. While the August Decrees were initiated by the unrest in the countryside, none the less the abolition of feudal dues was mostly declared to be conditional on compensation or purchase, rather than outright abolition. The destruction of the *terriers*, however, ensured that few of these compensation payments were made.

Much of the Declaration of the Rights of Man and of the Citizen was Enlightenment theory expressed in the form of legislative intentions. The prevalence of lawyers in the Assembly affected the content of the Declaration. Six of the seventeen articles were concerned with the law and the penal system. However much the French had a reputation for being litigious, the majority of them were not more interested in the administration of the law than any other aspect of life. Issues concerning punishment were the subject of intense debates, with philosophical and scientific discussion about the moment of death, and practical commercial questions (for instance whether a patent should be issued for the manufacture of the guillotine). Again, while the French peasants may have been pleased at the idea of equality of capital punishment, and beheading for all, it is hard to believe that they regarded it as a priority.

Enlightenment theory certainly dominated when the Assembly removed the authority of the Pope and made the Church effectively a branch of the civil service: the Civil Constitution of the Clergy was not a measure demanded, or indeed welcomed, by most of the French people, who had merely desired an end to abuses and the closure of under-occupied monastic houses.

The substantial laws about the future government of France put power firmly into the hands of the middle classes. Simon Schama's interpretation[1] is that the same people who had ensured that the Assembly would meet and take over full power were to ensure in turn that the power remained in their own hands: and, by 1815, the same groups were essentially established as the rulers of France. The regulations for election ensured this, since the measure of an active citizen was how much tax he paid. Throughout the whole revolution, attempts to achieve a universal suffrage, even a male suffrage, failed. Arguments against universal suffrage were well known and frequently expressed: that the system would be too cumbersome; that people who did not contribute to the public revenue should not directly have a say in how it was spent; that envy might cause non-property-owners to find ways of overtaxing the rich. Debates about enfranchising women and Jews were brief and infrequent.

Both local and central government was put into the hands of the property owners. In the new *départements* and communes, councils and officials came from the ranks of the active citizens. The brief period of central control during the Terror saw the power in many areas placed in the hands of the *représentants en mission*, all of whom were from the educated and politically aware middle classes. When local power was centralised, under the Consulate, the same class provided most of the prefects and sub-prefects. The methods of appointment might vary, but at no stage was popular government a reality. On the other hand, there is little evidence that the common people of France wanted power in their own hands. In any political system, the elected representatives are unlikely to be completely typical of their constituencies; and in an agricultural economy this is the more likely to be true: only exceptional, and wealthy, farmers would regard time spent away from the farm, sitting on committees and regulating schooling and street cleaning, as well spent. Michael P. Fitzsimmons suggests that the 'polity' which was established was in the hands of those most committed to, and able to implement, an equitable and workable system. Fitzsimmons claims that the institutions established were both liberal and effective.[2]

Certainly, opportunities were extended, with the abolition of class barriers to various professions including the armed forces. While education remained an unspoken barrier, in the army at least it was possible to rise from the ranks. This paved the way for a radically new form of army, whose welfare and career provisions were the envy of common soldiers elsewhere in Europe.

Equality of provision also improved the penal system: no one could be tortured, or arrested with undue force; decapitation as the only method of capital punishment ensured long debates to find an efficient and humane method. The evidence given by Sanson, the executioner, about the probable need to replace – or at the very least regrind and sharpen – the expensive sword after every beheading[3] may have rather a mercenary ring: but humanitarian arguments also filled the debate: the recognition that it took skill and training to behead painlessly with a sword was a potent argument in favour of the guillotine. According to Arasse[4] there were hardly any botched executions with the guillotine, in contrast to both hanging and axe- or sword-beheading, where skill plays a part. In this sense, efficiency and humanity were demonstrated by the Assembly's legislation.

The judicial system, too, became more open and accessible, for both lawyers and their clients, with a focus on local courts, and magistrates who were expected to have some knowledge of local conditions and no personal interest, in contrast to the seigneurial courts which they replaced.

This liberalism had its limits, however: attempts to end chattel slavery in the French colonies failed in face of the rights of property so clearly expressed in Article 17 of the Declaration of the Rights of Man; workers were forbidden from combining, by laws which were strengthened by successive French regimes until the 1880s. Plans for education and welfare remained at the discussion stage.

But, if the main need of the French people was for a stable financial and fiscal situation, the Constituent Assembly certainly failed. Their first measures, however popular, simply made a bad situation worse: they stopped collecting tithe, and declared that, while people should go on paying the secular taxes, these were unjust – hardly an incentive for taxpayers. The tax system which they put in place was belated, complex and unenforceable. The *contribution foncière* depended on the compilation of land registers by the new local authorities, whose members were, of course, anxious to remain popular enough to be re-elected. By May 1792, only one *département* (Doubs) of the eighty-three had its registers ready, and only just over half the communes had theirs complete.[5] During 1791, the total tax collected was 249 million livres, against an expenditure of 822.7 million livres.[6] Far more damaging to France, however, was the initiation and continued over-issuing of the *assignats*. Already by September 1791 the cash value of 100 livres *assignat* was down to 82 livres,[7] and this sort of inflation could only get worse. Florin Aftalion suggests that every problem in the Revolution has its roots in the *assignat* and the economic insecurity consequent on runaway inflation. While the Constituent Assembly could not see into the future, its members should have recognised that such an apparently easy solution as printing more notes would not work.

The Constituent Assembly, then, aimed to create an enlightened and liberal system, resting firmly on the good citizens of the property-owning classes. In doing so, it removed some of the worst injustices of the *ancien régime*, and accepted as a *fait accompli* the peasants' own ending of feudal payments and seizure of demesne land. It did not, however, address adequately the major financial problems of France, and many of its administrative and judicial reforms proved too cumbersome to survive the stresses of a long and difficult war: new local government mechanisms, new law courts, new crimes were all added to the constitution of 1791 within a year of its inception. Finally, in imposing the Civil Constitution of the Clergy, it alienated many of its citizens.

Questions

1. How far were the decisions of the Constituent Assembly determined by uncertainties about their status and the King's attitude to them?
2. To what extent does a study of the legislation of the Constituent Assembly confirm the view that these were 'middle-class measures for middle-class men'?

ANALYSIS (2): WAS THE CONSTITUTIONAL MONARCHY OF 1791 A VIABLE GOVERNMENT?

Monarchy was the form of government chosen by the Constitution makers of 1789–91, not least because it was the model that was believed to work so well in Britain. Several of the *cahiers* had mentioned the God-given status of the King, and only a few extremists believed that France could survive without a monarchy.

The King appeared also to have accepted the idea of constitutional monarchy. He appeared to listen to Mirabeau's advice that the exercise of limited power was the best way forward for the King and his (as Mirabeau hoped) chosen ministers. After his 'journey to Montmédy', as he preferred to describe Varennes, he seemed to have accepted his new, if reduced, position as head of the nation. It reflected the kind of reforming and 'well-beloved' role he had, at the start of his reign, hoped to adopt; besides, would such a loyal son of the Church have taken an oath with the intention of breaking it?

There were, however, several obstacles to the establishment of such a monarchy. First, whatever the King's outward attitude, he had not accepted the dilution of his divine powers. Those who surrounded him, and especially his wife, assured him that he could be restored to full power. He seemed unable to decide whether to take the advice of his official ministers, or of the 'court party'. The rapid replacement of one series of ministers by another was to be a feature of 1792. Meanwhile, he may have hoped for a return to his previous status: his brothers wrote from their exile that he should stand firm; the other monarchs of Europe condemned the rough handling of the royal family, and seemed to be on the verge of marching to their rescue. The documents that the

King so carefully locked away in his *armoire de fer* during 1792 were, according to Andrew Freeman[8] to be the archive of his version of revolutionary events, once he was restored to full power: letters from citizens and Churchmen alike condemning the Civil Constitution; drafts of plans for equitable taxation and justice, and expressions of Louis's concern that a few extremists were forcing change on his people. A constitutional monarchy could function only with the wholehearted commitment of the constitutional monarch, and that was lacking. The war, from its beginning in April 1792, served to worsen Louis's confusion and divide his loyalties; it also made his people distrust him and his Austrian in-laws even more.

Louis on several occasions demonstrated that he might have succeeded in the role he had accepted on oath. The people were willing to love him: the visit to the Bastille on 17 July showed this, at least according to Bailly's account; he and his wife shared the Tuileries Gardens, as they had shared the grounds of Versailles, with day trippers and picnickers. His behaviour in June 1792, when the Palace was invaded by demonstrators, was calm and even statesmanlike; but, too often he made serious errors in his perception of events and in his reactions to them: it had been Lafayette, not Louis, who had turned the ugly mood of the crowd on the night of 5–6 October 1789; the flight to Varennes, whatever he chose to call it, had permanently fractured the fragile trust of the people.

Louis himself argued that he could not be a monarch unless he had more powers than those allocated by the Constitution. Certain of his rights had been unaffected by change: he had full control over his own family, for example, where the King of Britain had allowed Parliament control over the marriage of his children. The Crown of France remained hereditary in the male line. And the King was to declare war and make peace. But otherwise, as the King himself wrote, he had 'but a vain semblance of power'. He had no control over money and a mere annual allowance. He could not choose his ministers freely, since they were not to be members of the Assembly; he had lost the prerogative of mercy, and any say in justice. His influence on legislation was to be a limited one: a veto lasting two legislatures, or four years. Louis's powers of patronage had also vanished, with the end of purchased commissions, venal appointments in all branches of government and the order of the nobility. In the provinces of France, the new electoral systems ensured that, as at the centre, the power lay in the hands of the prosperous and educated, rather than the King's intendants.

Historians from Goodwin to Schama have pointed out the difficulty of removing all the supporting and interconnected layers of the *ancien régime* while maintaining the monarchy itself. The Catholic Church and the monarchy were equally inseparable in France. Since the early sixteenth century, Kings of France had chosen the bishops of their realm, thus ensuring for themselves loyal propagandists in every diocese. The Church explained, week by week, that the King was anointed by God; now, elected bishops had merely to explain that the King was a servant of the law and the nation, like any other citizen.

The third ingredient weakening the constitutional monarchy was the development of a determined group who wanted either no monarchy, or a monarchy with no significant power at all. They recognised that the Constitution of 1791 was not a finished product, but a stepping stone. In 1792, Saint-Just was to encapsulate the views of this group: 'there is no innocent reign . . . every King is a rebel and a usurper'. Their arguments were that all kings must be tyrants, since they do not answer to the electorate; that this particular king was untrustworthy, as he had proved in June 1791; and that, in a France at war, leadership could not be left to a king whose loyalties lay, at least partly, with the enemies of France. The Republicans had many opportunities to gain converts: they dominated the Jacobin Club; the best-known journalists shared their opinions, and they controlled some of the most widely read newspapers.

Limited monarchy must always be a matter of balance, and requires commitment from all sides if it is to work. Whatever the mechanisms put in place in 1791, constitutional monarchy had too many enemies to survive in France. It is possible that, without the war and the associated focus on the King's loyalty; the system might have survived; but one of the reasons for the war was the hostility of the absolute monarchs of Europe to the system being attempted in France. Equally, it is possible that a greater commitment on the part of Louis might have made the transition to parliamentary rule a straightforward one: but character change on this scale was never a serious possibility. Robespierre was one of many who said, even before the Constitution was finalised, that it would not work. He was proved right, perhaps sooner than anyone would have predicted.

Questions

1. Did the powers allotted to the King by the Constitution of 1791 allow him to play any significant part in government?
2. Is it possible to apportion blame to one particular group for the failure of the constitutional monarchy?

SOURCES

The first group of sources provides examples of the legislation passed by the Constituent Assembly, while the second group focuses more closely on the status of the monarchy and attitudes towards it

1. THE WORK OF THE CONSTITUENT ASSEMBLY

Source A: the ending of feudal dues, 4 August 1789.

I The national Assembly destroys the feudal system entirely. It decrees that . . . mortmain real or personal, and . . . personal serfdom . . . are abolished without indemnity; all the others are declared to be redeemable, and . . . will continue nevertheless to be collected until there has been reimbursement . . .
III The exclusive right of the chase and protected rabbit warrens is abolished, and each landowner has the right to destroy and cause to be destroyed, solely on his own property, all sorts of game . . .
IV All seigneurial courts are suppressed without any indemnity, but, nevertheless, the officers of these courts will continue in their functions until the National Assembly has provided for the establishment of a new judicial system.

Source B: extracts from the Declaration of the Rights of Man and of the Citizen, 26 August 1789.

9. Every man having been presumed innocent until he has been declared guilty, if it is necessary to arrest him, all severity beyond what is necessary to secure his arrest shall be severely punished by law.
10. None may be molested for his opinions, even on religion, provided that their expression does not threaten public order.
11. Free communication of thoughts and opinion is one of the most precious of the rights of man. Therefore, every citizen can speak, write and print freely, subject to responsibility for the abuse of such liberty in cases determined by the law . . .
17. Property being a sacred and inviolable right, none can be deprived of it unless public necessity, legally determined, clearly demands it, and on payment of fair compensation.

Source C: Bill proposed by Dr Guillotin, for the reform of the penal system, January 1790.

Article 1. Crimes of the same kind shall be punished by the same kinds of punishment, whatever the rank or estate of the criminal.

Article 2. Offences and crimes are personal, and no stain shall attach to the family from the criminal's execution or loss of civil rights. The members of the family are in no way dishonoured . . .

Article 3. Under no circumstances whatever may order be made for the confiscation of the goods of a condemned man.

Article 6. The method of punishment shall be the same for all persons on whom the law shall pronounce a sentence of death, whatever the crime of which they are guilty. The criminal shall be decapitated. Decapitation is to be effected by a simple mechanism.

Source D: extracts from the Civil Constitution of the Clergy, 12 July 1790.

- Only one way of making bishops and parish priests will be recognised, that is, by elections.
- The election of bishops will be by . . . the electoral body as . . . for voting for members of the Assembly.
- Ministers of religion will be paid by the nation.

Source E: petition from Claude Louis Rousseau, a clergyman who had been a preacher at court, 30 May 1790. One of the documents found in the *armoire de fer*.

I was personally involved. . . . in the making of the general *cahiers*. Today, . . . it is with great distress that I see that several of the decrees of the National Assembly, no doubt against its intentions, strike a most cruel blow against the sacred rights of religion, justice and property..

Questions

1. Who formed the 'electoral body' (Source D) which was to be responsible for the election of bishops? [2]
2. What abuses of the *ancien régime* are being specifically countered by the articles of Dr Guillotin's Bill (Source C)? [4]
3. Analyse which social groups might be expected to benefit directly from each of the pieces of legislation in Sources A, B and D. [6]
4. What reservations would a historian have in accepting as reliable the evidence offered in Source E? [5]
*5. 'The ordinary Frenchman and woman was disappointed by the work of the Constituent Assembly.' Using these sources and your own knowledge, discuss whether this statement is accurate. [8]

Worked answer

*5. [It is important to demonstrate both your understanding of the sources and your own knowledge when answering these 'mini essays'. Since there is no evidence, except in Source E, of actual disappointment, use your knowledge of both previous and future events to help you assess the truth of the statement.]

The meeting of the Assembly was greeted with optimism by people in all walks of life; it could hardly have lived up to all the hopes placed in it. The end of feudal dues had been demanded in many *cahiers* and if, as Source A shows, the Assembly intended to be less generous than the peasants hoped, the peasants were well able to arrange matters for themselves. Freedom of speech and opinion were important to substantial social groups in France if not to all: the Protestant community, for example, had continued to suffer restrictions on their civil liberties. And the peasants, particularly after they had disposed of the feudal documentation, were keen supporters of the rights of property. Anyone who had suffered the depredations of State or army requisition and pre-emption was glad to have their rights to their own property confirmed.

Injustices in the penal system had long been a matter of concern, and both the Declaration of the Rights of Man and of the Citizen, and Dr Guillotin's Bill attempted to address some of these concerns. When the cleric in Source E complains, as early as May 1790, of assaults on religion, justice and property, he is speaking from the point of view of the privileged classes. The ordinary people were not enthusiastic, since 1788, about the Parlements and their stifling restrictive practices; nor were they sorry to see the end of the seigneurial courts. The idea of venal positions as a form of property was not of interest to the majority of the French, and so they would not miss them. As for the changes in the structure of the Church, we need to note that the priest was writing before the Civil Constitution was complete. Few villages actually relied on their religious houses any more; many coveted the land till then held by the Church. It took time, after July, for the ordinary people to realise that the Pope had been removed from his influence in France, and to worry about the spiritual implications of this.

These sources do not contain examples of the constitutional and administrative reforms; but these, too, appear to have been accepted by most of the French people. After all, anyone could aspire to vote or could seek to influence the electors, who were known in their area.

Some of the reforms seem rather academic and intellectual; and with hindsight we can say that the Civil Constitution proved to be an alienating factor for many villagers. Certainly some enlightened urban women argued in vain for women's rights. But, by the time the Constituent Assembly completed its work, much of France felt that it had achieved much of what was required of it.

2. THE CONSTITUTIONAL MONARCHY

Source F: from the Diary of Bailly, 17 July 1789.

As he entered the council chamber, there was a burst of applause.... And when he had taken his seat on the throne which had been prepared for him, a voice ... uttered this heartfelt cry: 'Our King, our Father', at which ... the cries of 'Vive le Roi' became even more intense. M. de Corney demanded that a statue should be erected to Louis XVI, the restorer of public liberty, and the father of the French nation, and immediately, by universal acclamation, it was voted that this statue should be set up on the site of the Bastille.

Source G: Louis's Declaration of 20 June 1791.

What remains to the King other than a vain semblance of royalty? ... The King does not think it possible to govern a kingdom of such great extent and importance as France through the means established by the National Assembly ... The spirit of the clubs dominates and pervades everything ... in view of all these facts, and the impossibility of the King's being able to do the good and prevent the evil which is being committed, is it surprising that the King has sought to recover his liberty and find security for himself and his family?

Source H: the Declaration of Pillnitz, 27 August 1791.

His Majesty the Emperor and his Majesty the King of Prussia, having heard the wishes and representations of Monsieur and of the Count of Artois, jointly declare that they regard the present situation of the King of France as an object of interest to all the sovereigns of Europe. They hope that this interest will not fail to be recognised by the powers whose help is entreated, and that consequently they will not refuse to employ, jointly with their above-mentioned Majesties, the most effective means, relative to their forces, to place the King of France in a position to establish, with perfect freedom, the basis of a monarchical government equally agreeable to the rights of sovereigns and the well-being of the French Nation ...

Source I: extracts from the Constitution, 14 September 1791.

2 The government of France is monarchical; no authority in France is above the law by which alone the King reigns, and it is only in the name of the law that he can require obedience.

3 The National Assembly has declared and recognised as fundamental elements in the French Monarchy that the King's person is inviolable and sacred, that the throne is indivisible and that the Crown is hereditary in the ruling dynasty from male to male in order of primogeniture . . .

13 The King may invite the National Assembly to take a matter into consideration, but the initiation of legislation appertains exclusively to the representatives of the nation . . .

19 The judicial power may in no case be exercised by the King or by the legislative body . . .

Source J: memorandum, read to the royal council by Narbonne, 24 February 1792, preserved in the *armoire de fer*.

Although royal power has appeared gravely weakened since 1789, it undoubtedly still has great influence, and could increase that influence . . . The Republicans can never hope to work harmoniously with the King; they want only to destroy his power. This leaves the aristocrats and the constitutionalists battling for the King's ear. The former have . . . an apparent common cause with the throne . . . For a long time the King has invited them to cede, as he has, to the changes dictated by the will which he himself has called 'national' . . . The constitutionalists are the authors or supporters of an order of things which forbids anything absolute to royal power, and for which the strength of prerogative has been decided upon by principle, and owes nothing to previous practices. The route that has been followed to reach this goal has probably often seemed more shocking to the King than the goal itself. Mistrust of the King's intentions is one of the Republicans' most deadly weapons . . . Ideas like those propagated by the Republicans are avidly collected by the aristocrats – they present them to foreign powers to oppose the King's official negotiations or declarations, and use them to inflame weak citizens . . .

Questions

*1. Identify 'Monsieur' and the 'Count of Artois' (Source H). What is the significance of their names being mentioned in the Declaration? [3]

2. With reference to Bailly's position and views, consider the usefulness to a historian of his account of the King's visit to Paris and his reception (Source F) [4]

3. Compare the King's view of his powers (Source G) with those powers as listed in Source I. Do you think his description is accurate? [4]
4. Assess the validity of Narbonne's analysis of the problems confronting the monarchy. How far does Source H support the point he is making about foreign powers? (Source J) [5]
5. Using your own knowledge and these sources, discuss whether the obstacles to the success of the constitutional monarchy were insuperable. [8]

Worked answer

*1. These are the King's brothers, the Count of Provence normally being referred to as Monsieur. They are important because, having emigrated in July 1789, they could lobby the rulers of Europe for action to restore France to what they saw as normality. Monsieur was also the heir to the throne of France in the event of the death of both Louis XVI and the Dauphin (it was he who became Louis XVIII in 1814).

4

THE WAR IN EUROPE

BACKGROUND NARRATIVE

The mood of the Constituent Assembly was pacific. Two declarations (22 May 1790 and 5 August 1791) renounced wars of conquest and declared that war, like poverty, was a symptom of tyranny, and that free nations did not go to war. This attitude changed, however, in the face of the threat of the *émigrés*, and of the foreign powers who appeared to give them support, for instance in the Declaration of Pillnitz, August 1791. On 20 October Brissot called, in the Legislative Assembly, for military action to disperse the *émigrés* in the Rhineland, and, from then on, speeches demanding firm action against the enemies of France became more common. Various groups in France thought that war would serve their needs: the Republicans hoped that it would reveal all the King's treasons, and the Monarchists that it would restore him to his place at the head of the people. Tensions in France increased with the King's use of the veto in November, and the change of ministry on 10 March 1792, making room for the Brissotins, notably the anti-Austrian hero Dumouriez. Attempts to make alliances with the 'liberal' powers of the world, Britain and the USA, were unsuccessful, and this, too, fuelled the anxieties in France.

At the same time, events abroad appeared to make war more likely: in December 1791, Austrian troops assembled to help defend Coblenz against any French attempt to dislodge the *émigrés*, and Leopold's death on 9 March 1792 brought to the throne the younger Francis II, eager to defend the rights of the Pope and of his aunt, Marie Antoinette. The diplomatic correspondence between France

Elsewhere in France, the most devastating and unpopular effect of the war was the levy of 300,000. The decision of the Constituent Assembly to abolish conscription had been much welcomed. The reversal of their declaration was unpopular all over France, especially in the west, where it began the long-drawn-out war in the Vendée. At the same time, the Catholic and Royal Army had other grievances, not directly related to the war. They had only passively resisted the Church reforms, but the death of the King, in January 1793, alienated the west of France permanently from governments in Paris. Was the execution of Louis a result of the war? Historians since Carlyle have agreed that it was: 'A King dethroned by insurrection is verily not easy to dispose of. Keep him prisoner, he is a secret centre for the Disaffected. . . . banish him, he is an open centre for them.'[9] If this is true in peacetime, it is even more so in time of war, when foreign powers would have welcomed a figurehead.

The fall of the Girondins was also a result of the war, and of their failure to deal firmly with the crises which arose from the war. The defection of their own hero, Dumouriez, in April 1793, brought into question their loyalty, and the subsequent federal revolts all over France demonstrated their inability to control even their own supporters. They could not collect taxes, or ensure adequate supplies of men and matériel for the front. Their rivals, the Mountain, could denounce them as incompetent and cowardly at best, and as counter-revolutionary at worst. Once they were overthrown, the Jacobins found themselves set on a path to increased *dirigisme* simply in order to ensure that France survived the war.

Questions

1. Do you agree that Louis XVI was executed 'not for what he had done, but for what he was'?
2. How far was the fall of the Girondins the result of the war?

SOURCES

1. ATTITUDES TO WAR

Source A: anonymous and undated memorandum from the *armoire de fer* headed: 'Observations on the speech proposed to the King' (by which he was to accept the constitution, i.e. September 1791).

The Princes are probably more seduced by the schemes of the hardline aristocrats who surround them, and by the romantic and heroic situation in which they find themselves, than they are by the foreign powers. How can Artois really be sure of the Emperor and the King of Prussia's true intentions? If, by some extraordinary occurrence, the *émigrés* were to come back, it seems to me that their predicament would begin the day after they returned to Paris in triumph. To conquer is not everything, one must then rule; to rule costs money. What will the King do with a nobility needing to be rewarded, with a clergy demanding all its wealth and land back, with the old financial deficit, and nearly two million livres worth of bad notes in circulation? Would he keep a garrison of, say, 200,000 Germans in his lands?

Source B: speech in the Assembly by Pierre Vergniaud, 27 December 1791.

The audacious satellites of despotism, carrying fifteen centuries of pride and barbarism in their feudal souls, are now demanding in every land and from every throne the gold and soldiers to reconquer the sceptre of France. You have renounced conquests but you have not promised to suffer such insolent provocations. You have shaken off the yoke of your despots but this was surely not to crook the knee so ignominiously before some foreign tyrants . . .

Source C: speech by Robespierre at the Jacobin Club, 11 January 1792.

There is in France a powerful faction which directs the manoeuvrings of the executive power with the objective of reviving ministerial influence . . . the leaders of this intrigue have been identified; their plan has been unfolded . . . I have seen in the conduct of the court a consistently followed plan for destroying the rights of the people and reversing, as much as possible, the work of the revolution: it proposed war and I have shown how that proposal is related to this system . . .

Source D: declaration of war on Austria, 29 April 1792.

... The National Assembly declares that the French nation, faithful to the principles enshrined in the Constitution 'not to undertake any war with the aim of making conquests and never to employ its forces against the liberty of any people' takes up arms only to maintain its liberty and independence; ... not a war of nation against nation, but the just defence of a free people against the unjust oppression of a King.

That the French will never confuse their brothers with their real enemies; that they will neglect nothing to alleviate the scourge of war, to spare and preserve property, and to visit all the misfortune inseparable from war on those alone who conspire against her liberty.

That the French nation adopts in advance all foreigners who, renouncing the cause of her enemies, come to range themselves under her banners and devote their efforts to the defence of her liberty ...

Source E: a letter from Chauvelin to Lebrun, 28 August 1792.

In general, if we reflect on the conduct of England towards France since the beginning of our Revolution; ... on her constant refusal to accede to the Convention of Pillnitz; on the declarations which the Elector of Hanover caused to be made in the German Diet when the question of the hereditary princes was first raised there; on the neutrality which England has steadfastly proclaimed, even at the moment when our troops were entering the Netherlands: if, to all these matters of fact, we add some reflections on her internal situation, on her commerce, on her finances, we cannot suppose that this power would be really hostile to France ...

All that England wants is to be respected, to be treated tactfully, to be left to enjoy in peace the fruits of her industry and commerce; and if circumstances are not at this moment favourable to the formation of close links with her ... none the less, sir, I think I cannot reiterate too often: – we must not for these reasons regard our relations with England as severed.

Questions

1. In the context of theses sources, explain the references to 'the Convention of Pillnitz' and 'the question of the hereditary princes' (Source E) [2]
*2. To which groups abroad was the Declaration of War (Source D) making a specific appeal? How effective would you expect this appeal to be, and why? [4]
3. Compare the oratorical style and the content of Sources B and C. How effectively does each put across its message and identify the perceived enemies of France? [6]

4. What reservations would a historian have about the reliability of Sources A and E? [6]
5. By making use of your own knowledge, discuss whether these sources provide a complete explanation of the reasons for which France went to war in 1792 and 1793. [7]

Worked answer

*2. [The first part of this question is simply comprehension; the second part requires a little analysis.]

The direct appeal was to anyone prepared to come to help France, as so many Frenchmen had helped the Americans. But at the same time they were appealing to the common soldiers of Austria and Prussia, by claiming that there was no reason for 'brothers' to fight each other; and, by implication, to those living under absolute monarchies, who might want to take similar action against their own tyrants. It seems highly unlikely that the appeal would have had any effect. The few foreigners who came to France were intellectuals like Tom Paine, who would not be particularly helpful in war. Soldiers of the armies in Europe were not likely to be able to make their own decisions about whether to fight or not. On the other hand, the declaration ensured that France occupied the high moral ground, so as propaganda for home consumption it might well be effective.

2. THE LINKS BETWEEN WAR AND DOMESTIC VIOLENCE

Source F: part of the Brunswick Manifesto, 25 July 1792.

... The city of Paris and all its inhabitants ... shall be called upon to submit instantly and without delay to the King, to set that Prince at full liberty ... their Imperial and Royal Majesties making personally responsible for all events, on pain of losing their heads ... all the members of the National Assembly ... And their Imperial and Royal Majesties further declare ... that if ... the least violence be offered, the least outrage done to their Majesties the King, the Queen and the royal family. ... they will inflict on those who shall deserve it, the most exemplary and ever memorable avenging punishment, by giving up the city of Paris to military execution and exposing it to total destruction ...

Source G: proclamation, probably drafted by Danton, 25 August 1792.

Generous citizens, all we ask of you is to be true to yourselves. We shall not try to conceal from brave men all the risks and sacrifices that your new enterprise involves. The French people are already confronting the Kings; . . . in this battle . . . the only choice is between victory and death. Citizens, no nation on earth ever won its freedom without a fight. You have traitors in your midst; without them, the struggle would soon be over. Keep united and calm. Plan your means of defence wisely and execute them with courage, and victory is assured.

Source H: extracts from a speech by Danton, 28 August 1792.

Our enemies have taken Longwy, but Longwy is not France. Our armies are still intact . . . The time has come to tell the people that they must throw themselves upon their enemies *en masse*. When a ship is wrecked the crew throws overboard everything that endangers it. In the same way, everything that might endanger the Nation must be expelled . . . The tocsin that will ring is no signal of alarm; it is sounding the charge against the enemies of the nation. *Pour les vaincre, Messieurs, il nous faut de l'audace, encore de l'audace, toujours de l'audace et la France est sauvée!*

Source I: *The Times*, 8 September 1792, but relating to several days earlier.

The people soon assembled in very great numbers in the Champ de Mars. The Municipal Officers . . . proclaimed in every quarter of the town that the country was in danger, and that it became all good citizens to fly to its relief . . . The mob proclaimed in answer to the Municipal Officers, that they had no objection to fly to the frontiers to beat the foreign enemy, and they wished no better sport, but first they would purge the nation of its internal enemies.

Source J: two extracts from the debate on the sentence of the King, January 1793.

Danton: I am a Republican and do not hesitate respecting the choice of that punishment reserved for Louis the Last. You ought to strike a terror into tyrants – I vote for the punishment of death.

Manuel: I vote for the imprisonment of the tyrant during the continuance of the war in that place where the victims of his despotism languished; and for his expulsion when peace shall be secured.

Questions

1. Both Source F and Source I refer to events in Paris. What were the events referred to? [2]
2. Against whom were threats made in Source F? Discuss reasons why these threats had no effect in Paris, and in particular, why they did not prevent the overthrow of the King on 10 August 1792. [5]
*3. Show how Source J demonstrates links between the fate of the King and the progress of the war. What other reasons might members of the Convention have had for voting for, or against, his death? [5]
4. Compare the tone and content of Sources G and H. Discuss reasons why Danton's approach in Source H is so different from that of Source G. [5]
5. Using these sources and your own knowledge, discuss the view that, within France, those in power made use of the war in order to achieve their own ends. [8]

Worked answer

*3. [This question gives you an opportunity to demonstrate your understanding of the different reasons for which people voted as they did in the debate on the King's fate. It is probably sensible to begin with what you can learn from the source, and then move on to other points.]

While Danton's main point is Republican, that kings should die as a matter of course, on the other hand he does suggest that death would be an object lesson to other tyrants, notably, presumably, those who were at war against France. Manuel, on the other hand, favouring exile as the best solution, recognises that, for the duration of the war, this would not be possible: presumably because the King abroad would strengthen the enemies of France. Tom Paine offered the same view. Some of the right-wingers argued that Louis should be allowed to live as an ordinary citizen, or, at most, be sentenced to imprisonment for his crimes. The debate also revisited the question of the ethics of the death sentence in itself (for example Osselin). Members of the Girondins were still suggesting a referendum, so that the people could decide, even as they voted, and Brissot argued as well that the tyrants abroad would be glad to have a martyr to inspire support for their cause. The left-wingers, on the other hand, all argued for death; some, such as Saint-Just, declaring that the mere fact of monarchy was a crime.

5

THE TERROR

BACKGROUND NARRATIVE

Terror became the order of the day on 5 September 1793, following pressure from the sections of Paris to 'give force to the law'. Bad news from the war, federal revolts throughout France, counter-revolutionary activities, not only in the Vendée and Brittany but also in Lyon and Toulon, treason even in Paris, where Marat had been murdered on 13 July: all these had convinced Parisians that a firm government was essential to the survival of the Revolution. It was clear that the new Constitution agreed by the Convention would not do for a country at war, and so it had been accepted on 10 August, only to be suspended. The government was to be 'revolutionary until the peace'. Although the structures were not fully in place immediately, from September to the following July the Committee of Public Safety effectively exercised control over all aspects of life in France. Some of the mechanisms had been established earlier, such as the *levée en masse*, a first Law of Suspects on 12 August and an attempt to control the price of bread in May. Representatives from the Convention had been sent into the *départements* as early as March, and the Revolutionary Tribunal had been established to deal with traitors.

Each of the twelve men of the Committee made his mark on the government of France. Lazare Carnot, the 'architect of victory', ensured that there were sufficient troops, adequate supplies and sound officers. Within a few weeks the war began to go well. R. R. Palmer describes the soldiers of France as 'unruly but patriotic, undisciplined but enthusiastic'.[1] The victory at Hoondshoote on 6–8

September, which enabled General Houchard to raise the siege of Dunkirk, was too early to be the work of the new system, but it was claimed as such; and when young General Jourdan forced the Austrians back at Wattignies in October, removing the threat to Paris, it was clear that the Terror was having the desired effect. Pichegru's victory against the Coalition forces at Tourcoing the following May opened the way to Fleurus where, in June 1794, Jourdan was able to achieve the full French repossession of Belgium. Military success did not, however, extend to the navy: the French fleet was again defeated, at the Battle of Ushant, known to the British as the Glorious 1st of June. The British victory was not complete, however, since US grain ships were able to get through and prevent acute problems in Paris.

Within France, Committee members such as Couthon, Collot and Saint-Just went into the *départements* to crush federal revolts and counter-revolutionaries. On 9 October, Lyon fell, and in December Toulon was retaken. Terrible atrocities in Nantes during November and December followed the defeat of the Vendéan army, and by the end of 1793 France was effectively back under central control.

Meanwhile, economic problems were being dealt with by various measures, of which the most radical was the 29 September Law of the Maximum, which was to be revised on 23 Ventose II (February 1794). These tight controls, together with the total prohibition on the use of metal money, brought a temporary stability to the *assignat*, and were enforced under the draconian Law of Suspects of 17 September: if the penalty for economic disobedience was to be declared a suspect, most citizens would obey the laws. The Committee of Subsistence, formed on 26 October, ensured both the food supplies of Paris and other big towns, and the provisioning of the army.

Dealing with the internal enemies of France was especially the work of the Revolutionary Tribunal: its courts dealt successively with supporters of the *ancien régime*, such as Marie Antoinette, who was guillotined on 16 October; with the Girondins, who went to the scaffold on 31 October; and with opponents both from the left and the right. The removal of the Hébertists, in March 1794, was followed by that of the Dantonists the following month. Police powers were increased by the law of 26 Germinal, and the

Revolutionary Tribunal was reformed by the Law of 22 Prairial, which declared witnesses to be unnecessary.

An indication of Robespierre's increasing authority was that by 18 Floréal he was able to set his mark on the issue of religion. The impulse of the early leaders of the Terror had been towards dechristianisation, expressed in the new calendar of 5 October 1793, with its emphasis on nature and civic pride, and the formal Cult of Reason inaugurated on 20 Brumaire (19 November). Robespierre inaugurated instead the Worship of the Supreme Being, with the first ceremonies taking place in Prairial. His growing power was, however, beginning to alarm members of the Convention, who overthrew him on 9 Thermidor (27 July) 1794.

Historians studying the Terror have focused particularly on whether it was effective in dealing with the acute difficulties confronting France, and on how 'terrible' it was for the citizens of France who lived through it. Since its purpose was to use drastic measures to deal with drastic problems, these two issues are the key criteria by which to judge it, and they are the topics to be discussed in the two analyses which follow.

ANALYSIS (1): HOW SUCCESSFUL WAS THE TERROR IN FULFILLING THE PURPOSES FOR WHICH IT WAS ESTABLISHED?

The purposes of the Terror were to bring victory in the war, to solve the economic problems confronting France and to deal with traitors and counter-revolutionaries. Robespierre, however, had a further agenda: to make the citizens virtuous so that France as a whole could become worthy of the high status chosen for it by providence. The effect of the steady increase in the number of ways in which a citizen might become a suspect was to ensure that the number of 'enemies at home' grew rather than declined.

In the war, the achievements of the Terror were considerable. From the panic and defeat which had been one of the reasons for the inception of Terror, France moved to confidence, and victory. Each victory strengthened the morale of the troops. The officers who remained after the mass exodus of 1791 were comparatively young and full of ideas. The men they led felt themselves to be different from the conscripts of the Austrian and Prussian armies, and, even when conscription was enforced in France, they knew themselves to be superior. Copies of the *Père Duchesne* (Hébert's polemical newspaper) were sent to the front to maintain their revolutionary fervour, but the fact that they were free citizens was emphasised still more by the twenty-five decrees and reports issued on the subject of the treatment of soldiers and their families, both during their service and when they were injured or killed, in striking contrast to the way soldiers in other armies were treated. It has been suggested, for example by Alan Forrest,[2] that this kind of care enhanced morale. At the same time, relentless measures were taken against would-be draft-dodgers and deserters.

The need for adequate army supply made economic regulation particularly important. Law and order were of course assisted by a regular bread supply into Paris, but the army needed not just food but also animal fodder, munitions and clothing. The Maximum made this possible, but at the cost of distorting the economy and, in fact, reducing supply at a time when the reduction of imports should have encouraged increases in production. Florin Aftalion[3] describes a range of adverse effects from this kind of *dirigisme*: producers' reluctance to send their grain to distant markets, where the price would be the same and they would not be allowed to add their transportation costs; farmers using Maximum-controlled grain, including even wheat, as livestock fodder, since oats, uncontrolled, rose rapidly in price; when house searches and confiscation became commonplace, the farmers reacted by planting less in the following season. Nevertheless, the Maximum probably did prevent famine. The *assignat* stabilised, but only at its existing low level, and only for as long as fear prevented people using metal money at the same time. Aftalion, from his particular perspective, condemns the Terror for its failure to make the changes which France had needed since before 1789: a radical and rigorous new taxation system, strict money supply control, an ending of the National Debt and encouragement of new industries. On the other hand, a country already at war and facing serious internal unrest could not really be expected to embark simultaneously on full economic restructuring.

Federalist and counter-revolutionary areas were dealt with efficiently and mercilessly. More than half the executions of the Terror occurred in the region of the Vendée; in Lyon, almost as many died as in Paris. Although there were a few sporadic attempts at risings after the Terror, for example the farcical Quiberon Landings of 1795, the acute threat of counter revolution was permanently crushed by Turreau. A combination of violence and propaganda brought other parts of the country under control. Couthon's demonstration that the blood of Christ, revered as a relic in Billom, was merely coloured turpentine, and Saint-André's new patriotic youth clubs in Brest, should be seen alongside the fusillades at Lyon, and the portable guillotine taken by Representatives on Mission to Alsace. There is no question that the Terror was successful in restoring order to the regions of France, giving the government sufficient control to continue waging war.

Dealing with the 'enemies of France' within Paris and amongst the influential groups at the centre was a lengthier process, since the criteria of definition kept changing. It would be reasonable to suggest that the Terror failed here, since the leaders of the regime were to meet their end at the hands of dissidents. The removal of the enemies of France was pursued diligently. Throughout the period of the Terror, new regulations speeded up the process: the division of the Revolutionary Tribunal into three parallel courts increased the turnover; the new police code of Germinal II enhanced the pace of convictions, as did the Law of 22 Prairial. At first, the victims were recognisably enemies of France, such as the Queen, or the Girondins. Rapidly, however, groups seen until recently as allies of the Mountain came under attack. Roux and the Enragés, who had spearheaded the attack on the Girondins, were soon removed, and the Hébertists followed. Their extreme views were not acceptable to the property owners of the Convention, and their removal was not opposed, despite the fact that Collot, Carrier and other leading servants of the Terror had considerable sympathy with their point of view.[4]

The attack on the Indulgents was altogether more controversial. Their views were shared by many, when they argued that, with the war moving to victory, France under the control of Paris and the *assignat* stable, there was no longer any need for Terror. Their leaders, Danton and Desmoulins, were household names throughout France: Danton had saved France when the Prussians appeared to be at the gates of Paris; Desmoulins had been the voice of the revolution ever since 1789. It was because they were so well known, and such good revolutionaries, that they were particularly dangerous, and had to be removed. Robespierre's hold over the Convention is confirmed by the very modest number of voices raised against the arrest and trial of Danton.

The death of the Dantonists removed the last remaining group of obvious opponents of the Terror. Had the regime been completely successful, their death would not have been necessary and the Terror would have ended, since emergency measures were no longer needed. But the Convention had declared revolutionary government till peace, and the French would not end a war in which they were advancing on all fronts. Thus the Terror was continued by force, and for other purposes than those for which it had been established, until fear and Robespierre's failure to read the mood of the Convention accurately, resulted in his fall and the end of arbitrary government.

Its successes had been considerable, although some of them were merely short-term. When Duncan Townson[5] claims that 'the threats to the existence of the revolution in the Spring of 1793 . . . had been removed or brought under control', he is writing of the short term only. Without the centralising policies of the Terror, France would not have mustered the strength needed to fight the European war: the Maximum fed and supplied the army. And, without drastic measures, the western part of France would have continued to be a source of weakness and vulnerability. But when the central control was suddenly removed in Thermidor, many of these problems re-emerged in worse forms.

Questions

1. What criteria other than its own stated aims might be used to judge the success of the work of the Committee of Public Safety?
2. Did the Terror come to an end because it had fulfilled its purposes?

ANALYSIS (2): HOW TERRIBLE WAS THE TERROR?

The death toll of the Terror, which appeared appalling to observers at the time, seems perhaps less so to observers from the period after Hitler, Stalin and Pol Pot, and the Terror has a bloodstained reputation which does not entirely match the facts. On the other hand, in many ways, the lifestyle which it enforced was 'terrible' for many of the citizens of France.

Their total number was not, perhaps, the most terrible aspect of the deaths in the Terror. After all, this was a nation at war, and people caught in armed revolt would be put to death in any time or country. The many thousands who died in the area of the Vendée and around Lyon would have been executed in any country in time of war. It was the deliberately horrific methods of death which made the Terror so terrible. The instruction of Turreau to his officers, to spare neither women, girls nor children who were found with arms in their hands, was equalled in ferocity by the methods used by Carrier to dispose of the counter revolutionaries held by him in Nantes. The image of people drowning as their boats were sunk, with soldiers chopping at the clinging hands, is an enduring and terrible one. The documents collected by Josh Brooman in the Longmans collection,[6] provide a chilling insight into the attempts to justify this kind of atrocity. In Lyon, it was for purely practical reasons that the fusillades were used as the method of execution, since the guillotine could not have coped with the large numbers. The effect, however, was designed to be a salutary one. 'What cement for the Revolution,' gloated Achard in a letter to Paris.

Almost as frightening for the citizens was the uncertainty: as the laws changed, so there were more crimes; because denunciation could be anonymous, old scores were probably settled; the Revolutionary Tribunal in Paris, after 22 Prairial, did not need witnesses, and even before that groups of prisoners might be tried together, and a single sentence passed. The presence of police spies in the taverns and coffee houses of the big cities engendered a mood of caution and mistrust, and neighbours looked askance at one another. The arrest of such former heroes as Hébert or Danton indicated that no one was safe, and arrests at dead of night added to the mood of fear and uncertainty. The guillotine itself was seen as inhuman rather than inhumane, its impersonal efficiency somehow making death more appalling. It must be remembered, however, that physical torture was not used in interrogation, and that, compared to some of the execution methods of the *ancien régime*, the guillotine was not entirely terrible.

Attempts to remove the legacy of centuries of Christian life in France were loathed by a majority of the citizens; but this alienation had begun in 1790 with the Civil Constitution of the Clergy. Half the clergy of France had refused to take the oath; now even the constitutional clergy found themselves treated as suspect. The worship, first of Reason, and then, by law, of the Supreme Being was alien to France. In some areas, a section of the population took to atheism with enthusiasm: in Paris, in Brumaire II men gave up their baptismal names in favour of 'Brutus', 'Marat' and even 'Pas de bon Dieu'. Dechristianising was used, in the provinces, as a weapon of State control, and the prohibition of the normal Christian traditions of France must have appalled the ordinary people. The everyday need to change the way they referred to days, weeks and months, the reduction in rest days from one in seven to one in ten, the requirement to work normally even on 5 Nivose (25 December) all these must have been dislocating.

The impact of the economic controls did considerable harm to the peasant communities of France. Production actually fell in many areas, with less acreage planted in the spring of the year II than in previous years. The revision of the Maximum in Ventôse affected the standard of living, since prices were allowed to rise to include transportation costs and modest wholesalers' and retailers' margin, while wages remained controlled. The National Workshops in Paris were popular with the unemployed, but they adversely affected existing metal and textile workers. By the end of the Year III, Boissy D'Anglas was to demonstrate that their costs were much greater than those of privately run enterprises.

Conscription was unpopular. In the first months of the compulsory levy, many conscripts had avoided army service, by bribery, by evasion or by desertion. The Terror imposed such firm control over much of the country that this was no longer possible: and the penalties for draft avoidance were terrible indeed. Once again, however, the experience of the *ancien régime* would have been as bad, since, at least under the Revolutionary system, members of all social classes might in theory be called. A country always short of funds continued to allow *remplacement* (that is, the right to send a substitute if the original conscript bore all the costs of his replacement), but it was not particularly common[7] because it was resented by the poor.

For some, the Terror was a splendid opportunity: 'Under the Terror, patriotism had become a highly lucrative profession.'[8] But even they were insecure. The poet of the new calendar, Fabre d'Eglantine, found his speculation in East India Company shares at least as fatal as his friendship with Danton. Even the most committed protagonists of Terror were discontented with what they had achieved. Physiocrats like Robespierre, or Carnot, would have preferred to let the market and not the Maximum run the economy; but the political risks of the inevitable rise in bread prices were too great. The extent to which Robespierre was the dictator he is sometimes declared to be is discussed very clearly by Duncan Townson.[9]

Although in some remote parts of France the Terror passed almost unnoticed, over most of the country everyday life was affected to a substantial extent. It was not, however, a complete and selfish dictatorship. The Convention continued to meet, and could have replaced the Committee of Public Safety at any time: and the Terror was finally stopped by majority vote. Compared to the worst excesses of the *ancien régime*, or, indeed, with the atrocities of the twentieth century, it could not be said to be entirely 'terrible'. On the other hand, seen in the context of the high aspirations of 1791, the Terror was a period of de facto collective dictatorship and its achievements are too limited to justify all the suffering.

Questions

1. To what extent has the 'Terror' obscured the real achievements of the Committee of Public Safety?
2. 'A panic-stricken attempt to control a divided nation': how apt is this description of the Terror?

SOURCES

1. MECHANISMS OF GOVERNMENT

Source A: extracts from the decree of the General Maximum, 29 September 1793.

All people who sell or purchase the merchandise listed in Article I at a price higher than the Maximum price fixed and published in each département shall, through the municipal police, pay a fixed fine, double the value of the object sold, and payable to the person denouncing them. These people shall be written on to the list of suspected persons, and shall be treated as such.

The purchaser shall not be liable to the penalty defined above, provided he denounces the contravention by the seller; and every retailer is ordered to have a notice board permanently displayed in his shop, showing the maximum or highest price of his wares.

Source B: extracts from a speech by Saint-Just in the Convention, 19 Vendémiaire II (10 October 1793).

. . . Bread given by the rich is bitter; it compromises liberty. In a wisely regulated State, bread belongs by right to the people. But if, instead of . . . putting pressure on the traitors, if, instead of paying for the war, you make new issues of *assignats* to enrich the wealthy still more, you are adding more and more weapons to those with which the enemies of France harm her . . .

. . . The plots, which for a year have torn the Republic apart, have shown us that the government was ceaselessly conspiring against the Fatherland; the eruption in the Vendée grew without its progress being arrested; Lyon, Bordeaux, Toulon, Marseilles all rebelled, all sold themselves, without the government doing anything . . .

The Decree on Government:
Article 1. The provisional government of France is revolutionary until the peace.
Article 2. The provisional executive council, ministers, generals and constitutional

bodies, are placed under the supervision of the Committee of Public Safety, which shall report every week to the Convention . . .

Source C: report from *The Times*, 20th November 1793.

A grand festival dedicated to Reason and Truth was yesterday celebrated in the former Cathedral of Paris. In the middle of the church was erected a mount, and on it a very plain temple, the façade of which bore the following inscription: To Philosophy. Before the gate of the temple were placed the busts of the most celebrated philosophers. The Torch of Truth was in the summit of the mount upon the altar of Reason, spreading light. The Convention and all the constituted Authorities assisted at the ceremony.

Two rows of young girls, dressed in white, each wearing a crown of oak leaves, crossed before the Altar of Reason, at the sound of Republican music . . . Liberty then came out of the Temple of Philosophy towards a throne made of grass, to receive the homage of the Republicans of both sexes.

Source D: from a report by the American Ambassador, Gouverneur Morris, 18 April 1794.

Both the Dantonists and the Hébertists are crushed. The fall of Danton seems to terminate the idea of a triumvirate. The chief who would in such case have been one of his colleagues has wisely put out of the way a dangerous competitor. Hence it would seem that the high road must be laid through the Comité de Salut Public, unless, indeed, the army should meddle. But as to the army, no character seems as yet to have appeared with any prominent feature . . . it is a wonderful thing, Sir, that four years of convulsion among four and twenty millions of people has brought forth no one, either in civil or in military life, whose head would fit the cap which fortune has woven. Robespierre has been the most consistent, if not the only consistent.

Source E: extracts from the Decree of 18 Floréal II, recognising the Supreme Being (7 May 1794).

Article I: The people of France recognise the existence of the Supreme Being and the immortality of the soul.

II: They recognise that rites appropriate to and worthy of the Supreme Being are the fulfilment of the Duties of Man.

III: They place at the highest level among these duties the hatred of bad faith and tyranny, the punishment of tyrants and traitors, help to the unhappy, respect for the weak, protection to the oppressed, to do all the good possible to others and to be unjust to nobody.

VI: The French Republic will celebrate every year the festivals of 14 July 1789,

10 August 1792, 21 January 1793 and 31 May 1793.

XI: Liberty of religion is maintained, subject to the order of 18 Frimaire.

XII: All gatherings which are aristocratic and contrary to public order shall be prohibited.

Questions

1. Explain the significance of *each* of the designated festival dates in Article VI in Source E. [2]
2. Study Source A. How efficient, and how equitable, were the methods planned for the enforcement of the Maximum? [4]
3. Compare Sources C and E. How clear a picture can be obtained of the changes in religion described in these sources? [5]
*4. Explain and discuss the validity of Morris's views on the position of Robespierre (Source D). [6]
5. Using these sources and your own knowledge, show the extent to which the mechanisms of the Terror introduced forms of government and control which were radically new to the French people. [8]

Worked answer

*4. [First, because the passage is quite a complex one, you are asked to demonstrate that you have fully understood it: this part of the answer can be quite brief; then you need to consider its validity, both as a source of evidence, and in the light of your knowledge of the period.]

Morris is reporting to his home government concerning the fall of both the Hébertists and the Dantonists, and suggests that Danton was removed because he wanted to share power with Robespierre. He does not make clear who would have been the third of the Triumvirs, though it was presumably not Hébert. Few historians would agree that at this stage of his life Danton wanted power: he seems to have been genuinely motivated by revulsion at the excesses of the Terror, and to have wanted to protect himself and his corrupt friends from the fate which would befall them if the Terror continued.

His suggestion that only the army could take significant action against the rule of the Great Committee was to be proved inaccurate in Thermidor; the army would not make its mark on the Revolution until the end of 1799.

Morris's less than enthusiastic endorsement of Robespierre as the one man able to keep the Terror in operation was vindicated in

Thermidor, when the fall of Robespierre, Saint-Just and Couthon was the signal which marked the end of revolutionary government.

Morris's known bias in favour of steady change and the previous, monarchial constitution does not prevent him being an astute, and centrally placed observer of the French scene, and so, while his predictions are not entirely correct, they must be of interest to the historian.

2. THE IMPACT OF THE TERROR ON THE PUBLIC

Source F: extracts from a speech by Robespierre at the Jacobin Club, 1 Frimaire II (21 November 1793).

... Some may say that I am a narrow and confined spirit, a man with prejudices, even ... a fanatic. I have already said that I spoke, not as an individual, not as a systematic philosopher, but as a representative of the people. Atheism is aristocratic; the idea of a great being who watches over oppressed innocence, is altogether popular.... If God did not exist, it would be necessary to invent him.... I repeat: the only fanaticism we have to fear is that of wicked men, suborned by foreign courts to reawaken fanaticism and to give our revolution a veneer of immorality, which is rather the character of our cowardly enemies...

Source G: extracts from a police report, Paris, 18 Nivose II (January 1794).

In the Rue de Saintonge, in the Temple Section, a little delivery boy, newspapers in hand, was shouting: 'Great denunciation of the Minister of War, who's given money to the *Père Duchesne*, but lets the wives of patriots die of starvation.'

Two men came up to him and, saying 'you lie, you are a ... scoundrel, no doubt paid to slander patriots', they kicked him in the backside and tore up all his papers. The child cried, but, when several people asked him what the matter was, one of them gave him a few sous and said 'Come on, don't cry and be a good patriot.'

... 'Lots of prisoners recently arrived in Paris' commented various citizens; 'to rid ourselves of them more quickly, they should be set up on the river bank and shot at from cannons.'

... Public opinion is entirely in favour of Camille Desmoulins. People are most approving of his last three numbers. No one hides the view that Hébert is no more than an intriguer, who is trying to make the people turn against the best defender of Patriots [Desmoulins] and that he wanted to slander Danton,

Philippeaux and Bourdon and other deputies well known for their republican virtues . . .

Source H: part of a speech by Collot d'Herbois at the Jacobin Club, Ventose II.

What have you to say about the confidence you have shown in these libels which disunite you . . . ? Don't you see that they are seeking to alienate you from the National Convention? What! . . . The Committee is accused of having spilt the blood of Patriots. They are accused of having caused the deaths of fifty thousand men! And yet you believe that the authors of these writings have written in good faith? You believe that people who translate the ancient historians for you, who go back five hundred years to show you a picture of the period in which you live, are patriots? No. Any man who has to look back so far will never be at the heart of the revolution. People want to moderate the Revolutionary Movement. Well? Can one steer a tempest? Well! the Revolution is a Tempest. No one can, no one should, stop its onward rush. Citizens, patriotism must always be at the same height. If it lowers itself for an instant, it is no longer Patriotism. Let us then cast off completely all notions of moderation. Let us remain Jacobins, remain Montagnards, and let us save Liberty! (*loud applause*).

Source I: from Robespierre's speech to the Convention, 12 Germinal II (31 March 1794).

The question is not whether a man has performed any particular patriotic act, but what his whole career has been like . . . In what way is Danton superior to Lafayette, to Dumouriez, to Brissot, to Hébert? What is said of him that may not be said of them? and yet have you spared them? . . . . Vulgar minds and guilty men are always afraid to see their fellows fall because, having no longer a barrier of culprits before them, they are left exposed to the light of truth. But, if there exist vulgar spirits, there are also heroic spirits in this Assembly and they will know how to brave all false terrors. Besides, the number of guilty is not great. Crime has found but few culprits among us, and by striking off a few heads, the country will be delivered . . . . whoever trembles at this moment is also guilty.

Source J: some statistics about the number of death sentences

(a) by social class

Social class	number	% of total sentenced	of whom women
'Sword' nobles	787	6.6	
'Robe' nobles	278	2.0	} 226
Upper middle class	1,964	14.0	137
Lower middle class	1,488	10.6	90
Clergy	920	6.5	126
Working class	4,389	31.2	389
Peasantry	3.961	28.1	281
Unknown	200	1.4	65

(b) by date

Month	overall number	overall %	Paris Revolutionary Tribunal	Paris %
Sept. 1793	72	0.5	21	0.3
Oct. 1793	179	1.3	48	1.8
Nov. 1793	491	3.5	54	2.0
Dec. 1793	3,365	23.9	76	2.8
Jan. 1794	3,517	25.0	71	2.6
Feb. 1794	792	5.6	62	2.2
March 1794	589	4.2	126	4.5
April 1794	1,099	7.8	244	9.1
May 1794	780	5.5	399	12.6
June 1794	1,157	8.2	659	24.5
July 1794	1,397	9.9	935	34.8
August 1794	86	0.8	6	0.3

Questions

1. Explain the link between the reference to Desmoulins (Source G) and 'The people who translate ancient historians for you' (Source H) [3]

2. Study the statistics in Source J (b). How do you explain the increase in the number of dead in each of December, January, April and July? [4]
3. How useful to a historian are reports 'from the grass roots' such as those in Source G? [4]
4. By considering the vocabulary, tone and content of Source I, discuss its effectiveness as a political speech. [6]
*5. Using these sources and your own knowledge, discuss the view that 'it was the ordinary people who suffered most during the Terror'. [8]

Worked answer

*5. [For 8 marks, it is important to make use of every source, using your knowledge to evaluate each.]

Robespierre's speech about religion shows that he was prepared to ignore the strongly held Catholic faith of the majority of the French: although he rejects atheism, he is more concerned with its supposed adverse social effects than with the needs of the ordinary people. The police reports show that people were frightened of the government but were not ready to stop reading the *Vieux Cordelier*. The fact that there were police spies reporting in such detail is an indication of the insecurities of life for the citizens. When the removal of Danton and Desmoulins occurred, the people of Paris did not prevent it, however much they filled the courtroom with their protests for as long as the public was admitted. On the other hand, they were happy to use the vocabulary of patriotism, as shown in the police reports.

Both Sources H and I show that the members of the Committee of Public Safety were concerned about public opinion, and they knew that debates in both the Jacobin Club and the Convention were widely read and discussed. They did not, however, take into account the views of the ordinary people about the judicial violence of the regime: 'striking off a few heads' was not the way multiple executions would be perceived.

The statistics in Source J confirm the statement very clearly. Almost 60 per cent of the deaths were among the peasantry and the working classes. Many of these were involved in counter revolutionary activity in the Vendée, indicating their dislike of the policies of the Revolution, but others were executed in Paris and other cities for economic crimes or for expressions of opinion which they themselves had not perceived as unpatriotic. Particularly towards the end of the Terror, when the federal revolts were a distant memory, the number of deaths mark a fearful attack on ordinary citizens.

The proportion of the much smaller privileged classes executed was, however, high. Fifteen per cent of the total executed were either noble or clergy, and comparatively few of them were trapped in the Vendée, or in Lyon. They were the victims of far more overtly political justice.

These particular sources do not deal with all the terrible experiences of the ordinary people, notably the conscription and the economic regulation which made life difficult for them. Nor do they show the sense of involvement which some clearly experienced in their section meetings. It is clear that the victories in the war, and the great civic festivals, were a matter of real pride and pleasure to many citizens, and these sources do not offer a picture of such events. For ordinary citizens, however, such public demonstrations could not have compensated for the dislocation and insecurities of a government determined to change not just the way of life but the moral ethos of the French nation.

6

THE DIRECTORY AND ITS ACHIEVEMENTS

BACKGROUND NARRATIVE

The end of the Terror was followed by a year of uncertainty. The loose coalition of the Thermidorians had in common only the fact that they wanted the Terror to end. Some of the most radical of the Committee of Public Safety, such as Collot and Billaud, joined with moderate members of the Convention who had been lucky to survive earlier purges, including Merlin de Thionville and Fréron, to bring down Robespierre and his regime. But finding a new structure proved less easy. The main aim was to avoid a renewal of dictatorship, and so the Law of 7 Fructidor II formalised the decision that the independent powers of the Committee of General Security should be restored, and one quarter of each of the great committees replaced each month. The first three members of the Committee of Public Safety to go were the left-wingers Collot, Billaud and Barère. After this, physiocratic principles were able more easily to replace those of *dirigisme*, and a moderate Constitution could be formulated.

A 'white terror' of violence against left-wingers erupted, killing hundreds; simultaneously, the counter-revolutionaries in the west sought to take advantage of the change in government. Both these problems were contained by a combination of compromise and firm action. An extension of religious toleration, concessions to the rebels in the west, a certain amount of condoned violence against the Jacobins and *sansculottes* were enough to enable the Thermidorians to turn their attention to Constitution-writing. They were lucky that the coalition abroad was very divided: Prussia and Austria were distracted by developments in Poland, and were negotiating the third and final partition.

Economic and financial problems were less tractable. The ending of the Maximum produced galloping inflation, with the *assignat* down to less than ten per cent of its value, and prices of foodstuffs back to eight times what they had been in 1790. Fortunately for the moderates, the *sansculottes* of Paris had lost both their revolutionary zeal and their leaders, and the famine-aroused *journées* of Germinal and Prairial (spring 1795) were suppressed with little trouble. The Thermidorians were thus able to hand over power to the Directory within fifteen months of the fall of Robespierre. Their new Constitution was a model of moderation.

A bicameral legislature, indirectly elected by active citizens, would be replaced a third at a time each year. The separation of powers, so much discussed, was achieved by the election of an executive of five Directors, one of whom, selected by lot, was to retire each year. Although the Directors controlled foreign policy, they had no control over the Treasury, which reported directly to the Conseils des Cinq Cents and des Anciens. Local government returned to the control of elected councils, although the Directors could send out representatives. In their anxiety to create a Constitution which would be immune from the risk of dictatorship, the Thermidorians created a system which was very vulnerable to attack by a strong and determined man. The right of the Councils to choose their own meeting place was used to good effect by Bonaparte in Brumaire IX; the fact that the two councils trusted neither one another nor the Directors, which also helped Bonaparte's coup, was in part structural and in part the result of developments during the four years of the Directory.

The first elections to the Councils returned a wide range of political opinion, including refractory priests and returned *émigrés*. The first five Directors included Carnot, a former member of the Committee of Public Safety, as well as the corrupt former noble Paul Barras. Their initial attempts to deal with the financial crisis were not successful. The printing plates for the *assignat* were destroyed in February 1796, but currency was still needed. The *mandats territoriaux*, issued instead, were soon also heavily inflated, and instructions that taxes were to be paid in kind or in metal money were mostly ignored. One result was continued hardship among the people of Paris, but the only attempt at insurrection was the desperate Conspiracy of the Equals. At his trial, Gracchus Babeuf was to use the defence that he had only talked, and had done nothing. But the rising had fed the middle-class fear of the left, however powerless and leaderless the poor in fact were. In 1799, the conspirators of Brumaire were to use the threat of a Jacobin plot to impose emergency powers and take control.

One contributory factor to the easy defeat of Babeuf was the good war news. From the spring of 1796, Bonaparte was sending home despatches recounting nothing but victories, culminating in the Treaty of Campo Formio (October 1797) by which Austria recognised all French conquests in the Rhineland, Belgium and Lombardy. The Directors had not authorised him to negotiate, but they accepted the terms, taking credit for a treaty which delighted the French. Their only remaining enemy was Britain, but, in their determination to strike at Britain's trade through Egypt, they attacked Malta and thus brought Russia into the war. The renewal of continental war placed an excessive burden on the finances, and their attempt to enhance the efficiency of conscription made the government unpopular again.

The annual elections of one-third in the two Councils proved to have a destabilising effect. In Germinal V, the elections resulted in increased right-wing representation and in strong opposition to the war. The Directors reacted with the Coup of 18 Fructidor V: 177 deputies were declared to have been wrongly elected, the Directors imposed martial law, and instituted military courts to deal with traitors and *émigrés*. They also seized the opportunity to take drastic action on the financial front: in Vendémiaire VI, barely a month after the Coup, the so-called Ramel Liquidation declared France to be partially bankrupt: one-third of the entire National Debt was registered as still being due for interest payments and eventual repayment; the remaining two-thirds was converted into securities exchangeable for the already over-mortgaged national property. This betrayal of the *rentier* class soon created a reaction. The elections of the Year VI showed a distinct swing to the left, with seventy regicides returned. Attempts to increase the income from taxation with new taxes were resented; but the most effective, and therefore most hated, law of the Year VI was the new conscription law, the Loi

Jourdan. The election of Germinal VII confirmed the anti-Directorial trend of the previous year, and was followed by the Prairial 'Coup of the Councils'. Such assaults on the constitution were bound to weaken the government, and, as bad news came from the war fronts of Italy and the Netherlands, various groups began to plan a coup which would replace the Constitution of Year III with a new and more centralised one. The choice, by the conspirators, of General Bonaparte to be their tool was to prove a mistake.

The fall of the Directory tends to overshadow its achievements, and historians such as Martyn Lyons[1] suggest that by this stage the French were numbed into apathy by constant change and therefore vulnerable to a military takeover. On the other hand, hard decisions were made by the Directory, and a start was made to restoring a workable and moderate system to France. The first of the two analyses in this chapter considers whether the Directory can be credited with any real achievements, other than foreign glory. The second discusses the reasons for the end of the last truly constitutional regime of the revolution.

ANALYSIS (1): HOW TRUE IS IT THAT 'THE ONLY SIGNIFICANT ACHIEVEMENTS OF THE DIRECTORY WERE IN FOREIGN POLICY'?

The achievements in foreign policy of the Directory are notable, but to claim them as the only significant achievements is to ignore other important developments. It can, indeed, be argued that the triumphs of French foreign policy between 1795 and 1799 were the victories not really of the Directory, but rather of their generals, and in particular General Bonaparte. We may also argue that the great triumphs in Italy tend to overshadow the less successful campaigns on other fronts.

These achievements were considerable, however. Austria was defeated and France took possession of all of north Italy, and tightened its hold on Switzerland. The British were now the sole enemy. Discussion about the costly and difficult nature of invasion of Britain, and the failure of earlier attempts to use Ireland as a springboard made the Directory reluctant to promise much help to Wolf Tone's United Irishmen in their summer insurrection of 1798. But to destroy Britain's trade would ensure their defeat in war, and to strike towards India seemed a daring and imaginative plan. Egypt held the key, and the declining Ottoman Empire would not be able to hold it. This plan ignored the overriding strength of the British navy, and considerations of geographical distance and difficulty, but the victory of the Pyramids appeared to confirm the optimistic predictions of the Directory; although Bonaparte and his army were subsequently trapped by Nelson's successful action at the Nile mouth, public opinion in France did not know of the setback. Meanwhile, however, the Tsar Paul I's romantic attachment to the idea of the medieval knights in Malta brought Russia into the war, and Austria also renewed its struggle, although both were easily defeated by the autumn of 1799. Meanwhile, resistance to French domination in Naples was backed by Britain, and at the same time a landing was made in Holland. Rebellions also occurred in Belgium and Switzerland, so that, by the time Bonaparte returned to France, success in the war was less complete than it had been the year before.

New taxes and a newly efficient conscription system helped to ensure that the army could remain on the offensive. Many of the taxes were unpopular, although the Directory stopped short of introducing a new salt tax; but they were necessary. A window tax and a tax of ten per cent on theatre tickets were recognised as taxes on luxuries. In addition, the removal of the weight of interest payments from government finances meant that funding the army was more manageable, and that the civil servants and other public workers, who had been without wages for so long, could expect to be paid. Ramel's plan for bankruptcy has been so frequently condemned that it may be tempting to ignore the fact that it was necessary and, in the end, beneficial to France.

Other achievements may be credited to the Directory. The fact that the Directory lasted for four years must in itself be seen as a significant achievement. The complexities of the constitution of the Year III make it appear unworkable, but the bicameral Assembly and the annual sampling of public opinion might have provided stability had circumstances been more favourable. The voters, whose wishes were overridden by force on several occasions, do not appear to have been prepared to protest about these infringements.

The Directory successfully withstood threats from both the left and the right. The Babeuf Conspiracy was potentially dangerous because the police legions, disaffected by non-payment of wages, and by the use of troops against the people of Paris, appeared to be sympathetic. There was no charismatic leadership, however, and Babeuf's ideas were too extreme to gain much support. Even their planning was inadequate, and the insurrection was over almost before it began. Meanwhile, the counter revolution did not revive, and, although the monarchy was associated with international peace, the Declaration of

Verona ensured that the King in exile stood no chance of being welcomed back.

Social reforms were bound to be a low priority in a nation at war; nevertheless, it was under the Directory that Dr Pinel first experimented with humane treatment for the insane, rather than allowing them to be a spectacle for curious visitors; it was also the Directory that began to implement a broad-based system of education, which Bonaparte was to adopt and then change radically to form the seedbed of his elite.

The achievements of the Directory are overshadowed on the one hand by the glory achieved by the armies abroad, and the rise of Bonaparte, and on the other by the fact that the regime ended in military takeover. Serious attempts were, however, made to overcome some of the most intractable problems facing France, and, for much of the period, to operate a Constitution which was – effectively – designed to maintain the rights of the people by preventing any faction from gaining power. While these achievements do not have the resonance of foreign victory, they are none the less significant.

Questions

1. Do you agree that 'by 1799, the Directory had shown itself well able to survive'?
2. Consider the view that 'the biggest failure of the Directory lay in allowing the war to continue'.

ANALYSIS (2): WHY DID THE DIRECTORY FAIL?

The Directory ended because it was efficiently overthrown by an intelligent and able military leader. Bonaparte had troops who were loyal to him personally; his brother was the President of the Council of 500, and the meeting of the Councils was being held in the suburb of Saint-Cloud, where the military could have a free hand. As Duncan Townson points out,[2] the citizens of France had become accustomed to seeing the military participating in government; they had been used by the Thermidorians to crush *journées*, and by the Directors to purge the Councils in Fructidor V. Similarly, the Directors themselves had enhanced Bonaparte's public status, glorifying his achievements in Italy to gain popular support for their war policy. They may have become aware of their own mistake by the end of 1797: 'the presence at home of so successful a general, who had more than once forced the pace of the Republic's policies against the instructions of its Directors, unnerved them'.[3] They sent him to Egypt in part at least to remove him from the political scene, but the early news from Egypt simply enhanced his fame. When he presented himself as the saviour of France, he was likely to be accepted. This interpretation does not, however, take into account the lack of reaction by the people of France, who allowed the coup to succeed, and Bonaparte to consolidate his hold on power without any resistance. It may be more accurate to see the Coup of Brumaire as a symptom of the failure of the Directory, rather than its cause.

The conspirators of Brumaire claimed that the Constitution was unworkable. It had 'no device for resolving an urgent clash between the executive and the legislature except force'.[4] But the main problem was that there was no political attempt to make the Constitution work. W. Doyle points out that neither the left nor the right 'had any interest in compromise or conciliation. Neither was prepared to recognise the good faith and legitimate interest of opponents.'[5] In addition, neither extreme knew clearly what it wanted. The right wing might want the restoration of the monarchy: but not the kind of monarchy promised by Louis XVIII. The left might want more central control, and an increased amount of equality; but not the rural-based levelling of Babeuf. The electorate had every reason to be unsure of the value of the regime, and apathetic about it. Their wishes had been persistently ignored and distorted, not merely by the Directory but throughout the Revolution. The annual elections, so far from allowing them to have the kind of government they wanted, merely reminded them regularly how they were ignored. As D. M. G. Sutherland points out, their modest aspirations ('order on the basis of reasonable liberty and civil equality')[6] might be met by a military regime as well as by the Directory. Indeed, once the Consulate was in place, over 75 per cent of its high officials were drawn from among those who had been deputies in the two Councils of the Directory.[7]

The middle-class electorate had, however, accepted the Directory for over four years. Only in 1799 did they allow it to be replaced, in part at least because it had made itself increasingly unpopular from Fructidor V onwards. The same traders who had imagined in 1792 that war would benefit them were now being impoverished by the British naval blockade. They wanted peace: but, for the Directory, war was an essential weapon of social control. Victory in Italy might have brought back to France not only the dangerously popular General Bonaparte but also thousands of troops, so the attack on Egypt was promoted as a step towards reclaiming the wealth of French India, lost in 1763. The resumption of a full continental war led to further civil restrictions. The Law of Hostages of 1799, together with the regulations against *émigrés* had a resonance of the Year II, and were not popular. But the demand for a forced loan levied on the rich was even more unpopular. The wealthy must have felt, at the time of the Brumaire coup, that those who were being removed had been too much inclined to the left.

The Ramel Liquidation had hurt many of them even more than the threat of a forced loan. Investments dating back to the *ancien régime* had been increased, in part for patriotic reasons, when the Republic needed help. Now the creditors were betrayed in an action which Aftalion declares to be 'reminiscent of the worse exactions of the monarchy'.[8] This betrayal of the *rentier* classes ensured that they would not rescue the regime which had taken their money.

For the rest of the country, the war itself was the main factor in the unpopularity of the Directory. The Jourdan conscription law of September 1798 affected almost every family in France. It replaced the haphazard methods of the past with a bureaucratic and efficient system. Every unmarried male was to be written on to the list of his 'class', or age group. Then, when the time came for his army service, the class, or part of it, would be called up by name. There was to be no *remplacement*, and exemption was therefore far harder to obtain, although Alan Forrest describes some of the ruses employed by reluctant conscripts, including examples of men in their twenties hastily choosing brides in their late seventies.[9] The calling up of whole classes, for example in 1799, was an early proof of the relentless efficiency of the new law. The fact that it was fairer than the previous system did not make it any more popular. A feeling grew that the war was being unduly prolonged, and many believed that the needless attack on Egypt was designed to provoke the British at a time when peace could have been negotiated.

It would be inaccurate to say that the Directory had failed totally: many of its reforms provided the basis for later developments: its work on education was more egalitarian than Bonaparte's subsequent revision. The regime attempted to develop a proper respect for State education by recruiting to the public sector only people who had been educated in the State schools or whose children were being so educated. This idealism was matched by commitment to technical and vocational education which Bonaparte inherited. New schools, however, were not enough to compensate for the unconstitutional and arbitrary behaviour of the Directors, or for their unpopular war and financial policies. It is ironic that it was some of the Directors themselves who sought to overturn the system, and therefore opened the opportunity for Bonaparte's coup.

Questions

1. Was the establishment of the Directory a step designed to reverse or to consolidate the changes which had been effected by the Revolution in France up to 1795?
2. Why was the *coup d'état* of Brumaire in 1799 successful in overthrowing the Directory?

SOURCES

It has been suggested that the Directory was doomed from the beginning. The Sources which follow consider first, the difficult circumstances in which the Directory began, and, second, various aspects of their policies and achievements.

1. THE BIRTH OF THE DIRECTORY

Source A: report by Barère, 28 July 1794.

Citizens, National Justice has triumphed . . . When one man despotically seizes the will. . . . of the most numerous, the most famous society of the people, he becomes imperceptibly the master of public opinion . . . When one man alone has in his power the influence of societies, judicial and revolutionary authority and military power, there is no longer any counter-weight great enough to maintain a free national assembly, an active and lawful government and equality before the law.

Source B: François Antoine Boissy d'Anglas in *Le Moniteur*, 1795.

We must be governed by the best citizens; the best citizens are those who are most educated and most interested in the keeping of the law . . . you will find such men only among those who possess some property, who are attached to the country that contains it, the laws that protect it, and the peace that maintains it; men who owe to that property and to the affluence it affords the education which has made them fit to discuss wisely and equitably, the advantages and the drawbacks of the laws that determine the fate of the country . . . A country governed by landowners is in a condition of social order, whereas one governed by persons other than property owners is in a state of nature.

Source C: Nicolas Ruault, journalist, describes the hardships of the winter of 1794–5.

The flour intended for Paris is stopped on the way and stolen by citizens even hungrier no doubt than ourselves, if such there be within the whole republic. Yet there is no lack of corn anywhere! The farmers absolutely refused to sell it for paper money; you have to go to them and take linen or table silver, jewellery or gold crosses, to get a few bushels. Discord sits more firmly than ever within the Convention. Now we are back to where we were at the end of April 1793, and a hundred times worse as far as financial matters go. Too many *assignats*, too much government slackness, too much favour shown to enemies of democracy, too much harshness and cruelty . . .

Source D: letter from Napoleon Bonaparte to his brother, autumn 1795.

The Committees chose me as second in command. We disposed our troops. The enemy attacked us at the Tuileries. We killed plenty of them. They killed thirty of our men and wounded sixty. We have disarmed the sections and all is quiet.

Source E: manifesto of the Directors, 5 November 1795.

Frenchmen, the Executive Directory has just been installed . . . Inflexible justice and the strictest observance of laws will be its rule. To wage an active war on royalism, to revive patriotism, to repress all factions vigorously . . . to annihilate every desire for vengeance . . . to restore peace, to regenerate morals . . . to revive commerce and industry, to revivify the arts and sciences, to re-establish plenty and the public credit, to re-instate social order . . . finally, to obtain for the French Republic the happiness and glory with it awaits – such is the task of your legislators and of the Executive Directory . . .

But . . . we need time, calm, patience and confidence . . . such confidence will not be betrayed if the people no longer allow themselves to be won over to the perfidious suggestions of royalists who are resuming their plots, of fanatics who are ceaselessly inflaming opinions and of public leeches who are always taking advantage of our miseries.

Questions

*1. Who were 'the enemy' referred to in Source D? [2]
2. What evidence is there in these sources to suggest that the left wing, rather than the counter-revolutionaries, were seen as the greatest threat to the stability of France in the Year III? [4]
3. By studying the vocabulary and tone of Source C, discuss its effectiveness as a piece of journalistic writing. [5]

4. Compare the views on what makes a successful government expressed by Barère (Source A) and Boissy d'Anglas (Source B). [6]
5. In the light of the other sources, and your own knowledge, comment on the difficulties likely to confront the Directory in attempting to achieve the aims set out in Source E. [8]

Worked answer

*1. [Do not spend long when only two marks are at stake. On the other hand, a one-word answer will be unlikely to attract both the marks. You might also want to show that you know the name given to the event: 'the Whiff of Grapeshot'.]

'The enemy' are the agitators demonstrating for further, and more right-wing, changes in the Constitution of the Year III, such as the removal of the two-thirds rule.

2. PROBLEMS AND ACHIEVEMENTS OF THE DIRECTORY

Source F: the Doctrine of Babeuf, May 1796.

10. The aim of the French Revolution is to destroy inequality and to re-establish the general welfare.
11. The Revolution is not complete, because the rich monopolise all the property and govern exclusively . . .
12. The Constitution of 1793 is the real law of Frenchmen, because the people have solemnly accepted it; because the Convention had no right to change it . . . because terror against the people, and the influence of *émigrés*, have presided over the fabrication and the alleged acceptance of the Constitution of 1795 . . . because the Constitution of 1793 has sanctioned the inalienable right of every citizen to consent to the laws, to enjoy political rights, to meet in assembly . . . to receive education, and not to die of hunger; rights which the counter-revolutionary Act of 1795 openly and totally violated.

Source G: the Manifesto of the Equals, May 1796, Gracchus Babeuf.

Equality! . . . Equality has been nothing but a beautiful and sterile fiction of the law. Today when we ask for it in a louder voice they answer us 'Be quiet, wretches! . . . You are equal before the law. Rabble! What more do you want?' What more do we want! Legislators, governors, rich proprietors, listen in your turn ... We will have real equality or death ... No more individual ownership of land! The land belongs to no one. We claim it back, we want the common enjoyment of the fruits of the earth.

Source H: a comment by Bonaparte, during his exile.

I came back from the Italian campaign with no more than three hundred thousand francs to call my own; I could very easily have brought back ten or twelve millions instead, and they would still have been mine; I never kept any accounts and I was never asked for any. I expected upon my return some great national reward; public opinion was all for bestowing Chambord upon me; I would have been very content to receive riches of this sort, but the Directory shelved the idea. Yet I had sent at least fifty millions to France in service of the State. This was the first time ever, in modern history, that an army has provided for the needs of the fatherland instead of being a burden upon it.

Source I: 'Each to his own bankruptcy', cartoon from September 1797.

Source: from the *Chronicle of the French Revolution* published by Dorling Kindersley Ltd

Source J: report to the Directors by a Commissioner in Seine et Oise, 1799.

They [the peasants of the area] are not in the least partisans of royalty, the memory of tithes and rents being odious to them. They are quite satisfied that their harvests should have doubled since the extinction of game rights, they recognise and greatly value the possession of equality. Many of them have bought national lands and all have improved their position, so that, when they compare the old order to the new, they give their preference to the latter. But the evils of the old order are far away, and they remember only the evils that have been brought upon them by the revolutionary turmoil. French victories appeal to a section of them, but do not touch them greatly because they are purchased at the cost of their sons' blood, and the peasantry are not sufficiently committed to accept such sacrifices. They neglect the exercise of civic rights because exercising these rights has exhausted them. They still give themselves to the priests more out of stubbornness than any other sentiment. This picture proves that it only requires peace, tranquillity and a certain period of calm to make them like the Revolution again.

Questions

1. Explain the reference to 'the Constitution of 1793' in Source F. [2]
*2. How far was Babeuf right when he said the equality under the Directory was merely 'a sterile fiction of the law'? [4]
3. What comment is the artist making in source I about the Ramel Liquidation? How effective do you find his cartoon as a piece of political propaganda? [5]
4. How reliable, and how useful to historians do you consider an official report such as the one quoted in Source J? [6]
5. Using these sources and your own knowledge, discuss the view that 'by 1799, the Directory had overcome many of the problems which had confronted it'. [8]

Worked answer

*2. [You need to put Babeuf's extreme ideas into the context both of the whole revolution and of the whole population of France to achieve a balanced answer. Note that he is addressing the legislators as well as the executive and the rich proprietors, and ensure that your answer reflects this.]

Equality before the law did exist, and it is a measure of the success of the Revolution that it was taken for granted, since it had not been a feature of the *ancien régime*. In other fields, however, inequalities still existed. Certainly common ownership of property was inconceivable: the rights of property were safeguarded from the Declaration of the Rights of Man and of the Citizen onwards. This benefited many of the peasants, who had seized land in the early months of the Revolution. There was no equality of civic rights, since only active citizens (defined by wealth) could vote, or be involved in government or local administration. Equality when it came to other forms of public service was also incomplete: although promotion was by merit, education remained beyond the reach of the poor.

7

THE
COUNTER-REVOLUTION

BACKGROUND NARRATIVE

There was opposition to the Revolution from the start. Within the Estates General, groups rapidly emerged opposed to all change, or favouring some kind of enlightened despotism. Papers were written, and plans made which were diametrically opposed to the intentions of the Third Estate. The Count of Ferrand, for example, published leaflets arguing that only by maintaining the three orders could the rights of every citizen be preserved. The court, and particularly the Queen's group, appear to have regarded these plans with optimism, but their hopes were soon swamped by the 'July Days'.

The first *émigrés* left France in reaction to the violence of July and September 1789; throughout the Revolution people emigrated for different reasons and at different times. By 1799, it is estimated that between 120,000 and 150,000 had left France, of whom 31.4 per cent left in 1789–92, and 68.6 per cent left between 1793 and 1799.[1] About 25 per cent of the total were clergy, and almost 17 per cent were nobles. Some *émigrés* left never to return. But an important contingent was determined to influence events, and to return to France at the head of a conquering army. The Count of Artois, from his base in Turin, tried from July 1789 to encourage insurrection in France. It was not until he moved to Coblenz in the Rhineland in June 1791, however, that an army began to be established, assisted by the mass emigration of army officers (about 10 per cent of the final total). Poised on the borders of France, the *émigré* armies appeared threatening. After January 1793, the Count of Provence declared himself to be Regent, and demanded the release from prison of the young Louis XVII. At the death of the young King on 9 June 1795, the Regent became Louis XVIII, revealing his lack of understanding of events in France in the Declaration of Verona on 24 June. A whole series of laws and penalties against the *émigrés* failed to persuade any of them to return, at least until Bonaparte closed the departmental lists and offered a welcome for Frenchmen prepared to commit themselves to his more monarchical regime.

Within France, popular counter-revolutionary feeling was stirred first of all by the changes planned to the Church. The deposition and execution of the King were perceived as further examples of Paris controlling affairs which should have been discussed by the whole nation. But armed struggle within France was triggered only by the demands of the European war. The announcement of the levy of 300,000 at Angers on 10 March 1793 led directly to the formation of the Catholic and Royal Army of the Vendée, and from then on a state of civil war existed. By 14 March, the town of Cholet was in rebel hands, and in June they took both Angers and Saumur, with their important bridges over the Loire. The reaction of the Convention was to declare war. Yet they still regarded the Vendée as a domestic insurrection, and thus felt able to use the paroled Mainz garrison against them without considering that they were breaching the laws of war. Between October and December, the Vendéans were defeated in engagement after engagement, before their army was effectively destroyed at Savenay (23 December). General Westermann wrote to the Committee of Public Safety, 'I have crushed the children under my horses' hooves, massacred the women. They at least will not give birth to any more brigands.' Figures quoted by C. Jones[2] suggest that 15 per cent of the population of the Vendée died in the war. The population of Cholet, the rebels' first stronghold, fell by 38 per cent, and Professor Jones considers the term genocide to be a reasonable one.

At the same time, Brittany was slipping into the hands of the Chouans. The government of the Terror ensured that main routes remained open and that the great naval base at Brest was still loyal, but brigands and Royalists threatened government agents all over the province. The Chouannerie hoped that the British could be persuaded to make a landing in south Brittany, link with the remains of the Vendéan forces and the Bretons and advance eastwards. The Thermidorian peace negotiators in the spring of 1795 were extremely conciliatory, and the agreements signed very favourable to the counter-revolutionary demands; but, if the government had hoped for peace in the west, they were disappointed. In June 1795, counter-revolutionary forces, convoyed by the Royal Navy, landed at Quiberon. The invasion was a disaster, however. The British, aware of its slim chances of success, declined to do more than disembark the troops, who found that the Republican government had been intercepting their despatches for some weeks, and were expecting them. By 21 July, the attack had collapsed and, while Tallien's Military Committee pardoned many Chouans, the 748 *émigré* officers who were captured wearing British uniforms were shot as traitors.

The counter-revolutionaries received little direct foreign help. The *émigré* troops in the Austrian territories were never accorded the status they felt they deserved; and while the British funded various spy rings and 'philanthropic institutes' to aid the counter-revolutionary cause, the modest amount of money they invested was matched by the imperceptible effects of these undercover activities. 'The British spy master, Wickham'[3] from his base in Switzerland, may have got information written in invisible ink between the lines of commercial orders and invoices; but by the time such information reached London it was presumably outdated; and the resources of the powers of Europe were sufficiently stretched in trying to stop the French armies' advances, without having spare resources for insurrections within France.

The Federalist revolts of summer 1793 and late 1794–5 may also be seen as counter-revolutionary. At no time, however, were the demands of the various regions uniform, or co-operative. In the west, royalism was distinctly a motive; but, in Toulon, the desire of the merchants for open harbours and regular trade was paramount. And in Lyon, although the citizens resisted the French government for some months and were brutally punished, no serious attempt was made to contact foreign powers or, indeed, other federal areas. These areas may have hated the government; but they did not long for the return of the *ancien régime*, or for a successful invasion by Coalition armies. William Doyle suggests that 'much of it. . . . merely sought to stop the revolution going further'.[4] In many areas, the peasants failed to support the risings, either because federalism seemed urban and thus alien, or because they associated it with their former seigneurs.[5]

Jacques Godechot's authoritative account[6] suggests that counter-revolution was neither sufficiently united nor sufficiently well armed to pose a serious threat to the Republic of France, and William Doyle makes the same point. None the less, successive French governments were clearly alarmed by the threat of the counter-revolution in its many forms. The two analyses which follow consider first the extent to which the threat of the counter-revolution was a serious one, and, second, the actions and reactions to the counter-revolutionary threat of the various regimes.

ANALYSIS (1): AT WHAT STAGE DID THE COUNTER-REVOLUTION STAND ITS GREATEST CHANCE OF SUCCESS?

To imagine a France in which the counter-revolution succeeded is to embark on what Niall Ferguson has called 'virtual history'.[7] There are, however, moments in the history of the Revolution when the state appeared more vulnerable, and the counter-revolutionary impulse stronger than at other times: the question is whether any of these opportunities stood any chance of being converted into success.

When the war began in April 1792, the *émigré* forces in the Rhineland were confident that France would collapse under the combined assault of their armies supported by the forces of Austria and Prussia. The French army had been weakened by the officer emigration; the ending of conscription left recruitment dependent on loyalty and revolutionary fervour, neither a potent motivation for rural France; and expenditure on matériel had been very slight, given the financial problems of France and the other priorities of the government. At first, therefore, the *émigré* armies, such as the legion led by Viscount 'Mirabeau-Tonneau', had some slight successes; but they were quarrelsome and disunited, with more officers than men in some sections. The Duke of Brunswick was reluctant to make use of them, and soon relegated them to minor roles which did not satisfy the ambitions of their princely leaders. As soon as it became clear, in the victories of Valmy and Jemappes, that France's armies could drive back the might of Europe, the possibility of an *émigré* triumph disappeared.

The eruption of the Vendée, and its early victories, seem to indicate that the Revolution could have been overthrown from the west. The counter-revolutionaries reached Le Mans, barely a hundred miles from Paris. Once outside their own province, however, the Vendéans failed to attract new recruits; their lack of formal discipline was more marked as their lines of communication lengthened. As William Doyle concludes, 'it seems doubtful whether the peasant counter-revolutionaries of the west, however numerous on their own ground, would have willing set out to march as far as Paris. And if they had, they would surely have been stopped on the way by the most seasoned and successful soldiers in Europe.'[8] On the other hand, the Vendée continued to be a drain on French resources.

The Vendéans might have hoped to gain support from those other parts of France which were in open, federal rebellion against Paris. The motives of the federalists were, however, different. The demands of Lyon were more for a Girondin-style decentralisation than for a royal restoration. In border areas such as Alsace, the complaints were against the conduct of the war, more than against the Republic. Although it took firm, and in some areas brutal, action to suppress these revolts, at no time did they appear likely to reverse the changes made since 1789.

The year 1795 has been discussed, for instance by Godechot[9] and Doyle[10] as the moment when the counter-revolutionaries believed that they might be close to success, although both agree that the threat was slight. First came the negotiations at La Mabilaie in the spring, which amounted to appeasement by the Republican government. The Chouans promised to abide by the laws of the Republic, and in return were assured of freedom of worship, exemption from conscription and substantial reparations for damage to property done by the Republicans. It is not surprising that the rebels became convinced that the French government could be pushed further. Then on 9 June came the death in prison of the young King Louis XVII. The report of his death caused a wave of sympathy throughout Europe, and the *émigré* community might have capitalised upon it. Instead, Louis XVIII celebrated the beginning of his reign by alienating many moderate Monarchists within France with his Verona Declaration.

The Quiberon landing was the last serious attempt by the *émigrés*; success might have been possible if the organisation and leadership had been more efficient, or if the British had been persuaded to allow their forces to land and fight under the command of Puisaye and his associates. Divisions in the high command, and the concomitant British mistrust, were, however, constants in *émigré* politics.

Within France, moderate Monarchists hoped that the Constitution of the Year III could be altered to include a monarchy; had Louis XVIII been at all conciliatory, the advantages of stability might have encouraged the Convention to place a King above the 'Cabinet' of the five Directors. In the event, the inept Royalist *journée* of 13 Vendémiaire (5 October) was easily crushed, and reduced, rather than enhancing, the popularity of the royal cause.

With hindsight, it is possible to say that the counter-revolution never had a chance of success. A number of conditions would have to have been met, such as unanimity of purpose, intelligent leadership, willingness to compromise, and consistent help from abroad. Lacking these, the counter-revolution was bound to fail.

Questions

1. Did the *émigrés* pose any serious threat to the French Revolutionary governments?
2. How much support did the counter-revolution have within France?

ANALYSIS (2): HOW FAR DID FEAR OF COUNTER-REVOLUTION AFFECT THE POLICIES OF SUCCESSIVE FRENCH GOVERNMENTS FROM 1790 TO 1802?

Throughout the Revolution, the counter-revolutionaries were seen as a serious threat, and on several occasions governments appear to have been convinced that, unless they took strong action, the Revolution would be defeated by force of arms within France. The methods they adopted ranged from total war to complete appeasement. At the same time, the ways in which the loyally Republican areas of France were governed were affected by official fear of counter-revolution. In turn, the often repressive laws had the effect of alienating new groups, who might join one of the many counter-revolutionary movements.

Debates of the Constituent Assembly in 1790 and 1791 were coloured by the knowledge that the *émigré* princes were against the King signing any new constitution. The early promulgation of the Declaration of the Rights of Man ensured that, if France were to lose its newly tasted freedom to a restored absolute monarch, the established ideals of the Revolution could be used as a rallying point. Every limitation on the King's power was justified by the possibility that he might use any power he had to help the counter-revolution. The Civil Constitution of the Clergy recognised and attempted to harness the great influence that the Church had over the minds of rural French people. It is ironic that this and later assaults on the Catholic Church should have been such a powerful recruiting force for the counter-revolution.

The 1792 declaration of war arose in part from the exaggerated fear of the émigrés expressed in the speeches of the left. A beleaguered republic, with its most determined enemies at its borders, had no choice but to go to war. And, once the war had begun, war-winning policies had to be adopted, including the levy which ignited civil war in the Vendée. Laws of increasing virulence were issued against the émigrés from December 1790 onwards. Each département was required to keep a list of émigrés, although, as Godechot demonstrates, they were not always accurate, whether by incompetence or by design.

The French government was also concerned about traitors within Republican France. The hysteria which followed the defection of Lafayette, in August 1792, led to tight controls on suspects, and was one of the reasons why the Paris prisons were full of priests. The September Massacres of which these priests were the victims were therefore the result of the fear of counter-revolution. Every subsequent disaster or rumour of defeat led to increased vigilance against suspects. On 17 September, the Great Law of Suspects defined six different types of suspicious behaviour, including 'talking in an aristocratic way'. The detention of suspects, at their own expense, was recognised as an unjust, though necessary, policy in time of national crisis. But once suspects were in custody, it was comparatively easy to find or fabricate evidence of a crime, and place them before the Revolutionary Tribunal, accused of treason.

The Terror was the most significant reaction to the counter-revolutionary threat. With traitors everywhere, with large areas of France refusing to obey the people's government, firm action was perceived as essential, and, from September 1793 to July 1794, counter-revolution was crushed wherever it appeared. It seems unlikely that the foreign war alone would have been adequate justification for the period of dictatorship which the Convention accepted and endorsed: it was a weapon against counter-revolution. The Law of the Maximum, the end of the right of insurrection, censorship of the press, the closure of the Vieux Cordelier all these were declared to be attempts to defeat a far-reaching conspiracy. By July 1794, France was united in republicanism; the coup of Thermidor would not have happened if the conspirators had feared an assault from the west, or renewed federal revolt.

The Thermidorians knew that counter-revolution might erupt again once the iron hand of the Terror had been removed. Their policies were diametrically opposed to those of the Terror. Concessions on religion were made to the whole of France, and the Maximum was allowed to collapse; but especially favourable terms were negotiated with the rebels in the west, although, when the Chouans attempted one last rising, in June 1795, the Thermidorians demonstrated that they were perfectly capable of decisive action. At the same time, the new constitution of the Year III was designed, in part at least, to placate those who believed that France would be better ruled by men of substance, and with a clear hierarchy of power.

The right greeted with optimism the establishment of the Directory. Annual elections would reveal the true wishes of the propertied classes, and would, they believed, soon fill both Councils with representatives keen to vote for the restoration of the monarchy and of the Roman Church. They were to be disappointed. Although the west of France had been more or less peaceful since Quiberon, General Hoche still had troops based there, and the counter-revolutionary leaders Charette and Stofflet were captured and killed before they could renew the armed struggle. Louis XVIII was encouraged by Bonaparte's coup, and wrote to him in February 1800, 'Save France from her passions and you will have fulfilled my heart's desire. Restore her King to her and future generations will bless your memory.' Bonaparte replied, some months later, 'You must not hope for your return to France.' The Consulate was not a step towards the restoration of the Bourbons.

Throughout the Revolutionary period, then, French governments reacted to the threat, real or perceived, of counter-revolution. Many of their most extreme laws and regulations were enacted to combat treason and rebellion. If there had been general acceptance of the Revolutionary changes through all classes and all regions of France, it is reasonable to suppose that the Constitution of 1791 might have remained in force, and a limited monarchy might have been established in France.

Questions

1. How true is it to say that the Civil Constitution of the Clergy was the main cause of the growth of counter-revolutionary activity?

2. How does an understanding of the counter-revolution help to explain the onset and violent nature of the Terror?

SOURCES

The sources in this chapter have been chosen to illustrate a range of aspects of the counter-revolution. The first group is concerned with the different branches of the movement, and the second with Republican reactions to it.

1. ASPECTS OF COUNTER-REVOLUTION

Source A: letter from the Count of Provence to his brother the Count of Artois, 28 January 1793.

. . . it is to restore the throne of the King to our nephew and lord, to seat him and maintain him upon it, and to re-integrate him in the possession of all the rights of his crown that we summon you to assist us, you Charles Philippe of France, Comte d'Artois.

Source B: 'Address to the French' written by Abbé Bernier, May 1793.

Heaven has declared for the holiest and most just of causes . . . We know the true wish of France . . . namely to recover and preserve for ever our holy apostolic and Roman Catholic religion. It is to have a King who will serve as father within and protector without . . .

Patriots, our enemies, you accuse us of overturning our *patrie* by rebellion, but it is you who, subverting all the principles of the religious and political order, were the first to proclaim that insurrection is the most sacred of duties. You have introduced atheism in the place of religion, anarchy in the place of laws, men who are tyrants in the place of the King who was our father. You reproach us with religious fanaticism, you whose pretensions to liberty have led to the most extreme penalties.

Source C: extract from Joseph Farington's Diary, 21 July 1793.

At Richmond . . . there are a great number of French Emigrants, many of them of high fashion. That party spirit rages among them, some being royalists, others as they call themselves Constitutionalists, which makes it necessary to be cautious not to assemble them together, though they labour under the common grievance of being expelled from their native country.

Source D: a peasant's contemporary account of the warfare in the Vendée.

Our army consisted of peasants like myself, wearing smocks or rough coats, armed with shotguns, pistols, muskets, often with tools – scythes, cudgels, axes, knives and roasting spits. It was organised by parish and district, under the orders of an individual leader. We would march straight to the enemy, and, having knelt to receive our priest's blessing, we would open fire at point blank range, no doubt rather irregular, but well sustained and well aimed. As soon as we saw the Republican gunners about to open fire we would fling ourselves flat on the ground. When the shot had passed without hitting us we would get up and rush on the gun batteries like lightning so as to seize them before they had time to reload the guns.

Source E: memoirs of Mme la Marquise de Rochejacquelin, published in 1817.

The generals resolved to conquer or die in the coming engagement. The atrocities committed by the 'Blues' had infuriated everyone. It was decided that no prisoners should be taken, and that the soldiers from Mainz should be regarded as having violated the clause in the treaty by which they had undertaken not to fight for a year against the allies – a clause which implicitly included the Vendée, as that region provided the loyal and lawful army of the King of France and his contingent in the coalition. Consequently it was forbidden to call for surrender . . .

The march of the army of the Vendée provided a strange spectacle. The advance guard was fairly powerful and was provided with a few cannon. After them came . . . a disorderly throng which filled up the whole road. In the confused mass one could pick out the artillery, baggage trains, women carrying their children, old men helped along by their sons, wounded men dragging themselves along with difficulty and a random assemblage of soldiers . . . This melancholy procession was usually strung out over a distance of four leagues . . . What preserved our army for so long was the mistaken habit of the Republicans of always attacking the head or the tail of the column . . .

Questions

1. Who were the Counts of Provence and Artois (Source A)? [2]
2. Does Source B provide a complete summary of the views and aims of the counter-revolution? [5]

*3. The memoirs from which Source E were taken were published in 1817. What evidence is there in the extract as to the date about which she is writing? [5]
4. How useful to a historian is an anonymous account such as Source D? [5]
5. Using these sources and your own knowledge, discuss the extent to which the counter-revolution posed a real threat to Revolutionary France. [8]

Worked answer

*3. [It is important to 'earn' all five of the marks, and this is best done by finding several different pointers within the extract and demonstrating your knowledge, to help you reach your conclusion.]

The author of these memoirs is an authoritative source, having been married first to General Lescure (who died of wounds after Cholet) and then to General Henri de Rochejacquelin, who was killed in February 1794; thus she knew about events in the Vendée
Clearly this source does not refer to the beginning of the Vendéan conflict, since the author is describing an army with wounded men, and the straggling progress of retreat. She also writes about the habit of the Republicans of 'always' attacking at the head or tail of the column. There are, however, clearer pointers to the precise date she is referring to. The reference to the atrocities may well refer to Westermann's behaviour after Savenay (December 1793) about which he wrote, 'I have crushed the children under my horses' hooves, massacred the women. They at least will not give birth to any more brigands.' The most specific information concerns the Mainz soldiers, which provides an exact 'earliest' date for this passage. The Mainz garrison surrendered to the Prussians on 23 July 1793 and were released on parole, having committed themselves not to fight against the Coalition powers. They were used in the Vendée from August onwards, with the Republican justification that the Vendée was a domestic issue, rather than a part of the international war.

It seems probable, therefore, that the passage refers to the winter and spring of 1793–4.

2. REPUBLICAN RESPONSES TO THE COUNTER-REVOLUTION

Source F: Brissot in the Legislative Assembly, 1791.

Do you wish at one blow to destroy the aristocracy, the refractory priests, the malcontents? . . . Then destroy Coblenz. The Head of the nation will then be obliged to reign in accordance with the Constitution . . .

Source G: Collot d'Herbois to Duplay in Paris, from Commune Affranchie (Lyon) 15 Frimaire II (5 December 1793).

We have created a commission which judges traitors as promptly as would a true republican conscience. Sixty-four conspirators were shot yesterday at the very place where they fired upon the patriots. Two hundred and thirty-four will fall today in the execrable redoubt that belched forward death upon the republican army. Such examples will influence the cities that waver.

Source H: from the memoirs of General Turreau, published in 1824.

The Vendéans possessed a hitherto unknown style of fighting and an inimitable one, in that it was solely appropriate to the country and . . . its inhabitants. They were unshakeably attached to their political ideals, possessed unlimited confidence in their chiefs and kept their promises with a loyalty which could serve as a substitute for discipline. Their courage was indomitable, proof against danger, hardship and privation . . . animated at once by the spirit of religion and royalism, these Frenchmen, who for long preserved a record of victory, could only be conquered by French Republicans . . .

Generally speaking, warfare in the Vendée possesses such singular characteristics that it needs long experience to master them, and the skilful general arriving with ten frontier campaigns to his credit will find it very difficult to operate successfully in this region. Let [my fellow generals] say if they know of any form of war more cruel and exacting for soldiers of every rank, and more bloody than this. Will they not agree with me when I say it kills order, discipline and subordination in the army, and that the French soldier, speedily softened and debased in a country whose pestiferous climate seems to taint the moral complexion of those who approach it . . . disgusted at a war in which no glory is to be won, soon loses the energy, the constancy and the unconquerable courage, which have brought him countless victories over the soldiers of England and Austria?

Source I: proclamation of the Catholic and Royal Army of Brittany to the inhabitants of La Prevalaye, 21 April 1795.

We have pleaded your interests. We have obtained from the representatives of the people their promise . . . you can be certain that they are going to unite at our request to re-establish happiness throughout your countryside. Prisons in future will be only for wrongdoers; your property and your persons are made sacred by the law; all your sacrifices will have their record . . . We must now think only of the common markets and of provisioning and exchange.

Source J: letter from Charette about the Treaty of Mabilais, May 1795.

Tell the British government and the Princes that I signed the peace simply because I feared that my party, given its total lack of powder, would be destroyed in an assault that was being prepared by superior forces: but assure them that I will never make a genuine peace with those who have murdered my King and my country . . . I am entirely ready to take up arms again. My soldiers are battle-hardened and eager to fight; it is simply prudence which leads me to hold them back until I can fight with advantage.

Questions

1. Explain the reference to 'Coblenz' in Source F. [2]
2. By commenting on the tone and content of Collot d'Herbois's letter, Source G, discuss how effective a piece of political writing it is. [4]
3. How convincing are the reasons identified by Turreau (Source H) for the limited success of Republican armies in the Vendée? [5]
*4. Compare the attitudes of Sources I and J to the negotiations with the Republicans. What light do these sources shed on the difficulties of achieving peace? [6]
5. 'Successive French governments overreacted to the dangers of Counter Revolution.' Using these sources and your own knowledge, analyse the truth of this statement. [8]

Worked answer

*4. [You should compare the circumstances and purposes of the two sources, as well as their content.]

Source I is a public declaration, intended to convince the mass of the population that they are not being betrayed, while Source J is a private refutation of a solemn public commitment. Thus I appears to believe in Republican good faith, while J is a cynical rejection of a previous sworn commitment. Source I uses the respectful term 'the representatives of the people', while Source J describes the Republicans as 'those who have murdered my King and my country'. The divisions among the counter-revolutionary leaders, and their differing attitudes to peace-making, made any negotiation inevitably incomplete and unreliable.

Source I emphasises the economic needs of the region, and the commercial benefits likely to flow from peace; J is dealing purely with the military aspect, as if the only problem facing the counter-revolutionary struggle was a shortage of war matériel, specifically powder. He exaggerates the strength of his forces to drive home this point.

The fact that the rebels in the west were in contact with Britain, and with the *émigré* court, as demonstrated in Source J, was known to the Republican government and made them very anxious. Of course, they were right not to trust the signatories of the Treaty, since the landings at Quiberon Bay occurred in June 1795; on the other hand, the failure of those landings confirmed the impression given in I, rather than J, of the overall weakness of the Royalist cause by 1795.

8

DID THE FRENCH REVOLUTION END WITH BONAPARTE?

BACKGROUND NARRATIVE

By the autumn of 1799, a substantial group of influential people had determined that the Directory should end. As at Thermidor, a bizarre mixture of idealists like Sieyès and corrupt pragmatists such as Barras came together. The mechanism they planned to adopt was to harness the fear which the Jacobins still inspired. The supposed threat of left-wing plots justified the summoning of army units to protect the Councils, and their relocation, out of the dangerous centre of Paris to the quiet suburb of Saint-Cloud. It seems strange that none of the astute conspirators had guessed that Bonaparte would use his forces to seize power for himself, but they clearly underestimated him.

The new Constitution of the Year VIII (December 1799) put the power into the hands of a First Consul, advised by two others. A legislative body, with two parts, and a Council of State had little popular representation, since the First Consul initiated all legislation. The renewable term of the consuls was to be ten years, but in 1802 Bonaparte declared himself First Consul for life. His new local government structure maintained the *départements* and communes, turning them into agencies of central control, with centrally appointed prefects and mayors. These local officials administered the law, and the codifying of both civil and criminal law was one of Bonaparte's most lasting achievements. His reforms in education, similarly, introduced a uniform system across France, with the departmental *lycées* selecting the very best for advanced education. A single university of France, with branches on the sites of the ancient universities of France, as well as the new technical and specialist institutions of the Directory, was controlled and united by centrally ordained curricula and close supervision.

The Revolutionary changes in religion, which had so divided France, were, to an extent, reversed by Bonaparte. His negotiations with the Pope were so skilfully accomplished that, by the time the Pontiff realised how little he had gained, it was too late: Catholicism became the religion of the majority of the French; but the confiscated property of the Church was not returned and the Organic Articles ensured that any power remained with the First Consul, who paid and therefore controlled the clergy.

The Directory had begun the radical steps necessary to sort out the finances of France. Bonaparte built upon their work, setting up the Bank of France to administer public borrowing and collecting taxes more efficiently than had been achieved even during the Terror. Aggressive pursuit of war profiteers, such as Ouvrard, together with relentless collection of arrears of tax by Gaudin, once employed by the Royal Treasury, meant that for some years the Consulate was able to balance its books. The war, of course, put an end to this financial stability. As soon as he came to power, Bonaparte had embarked on a rapid and efficient campaign against the Austrians in the north of Italy, and, by the spring of 1802, there was peace, even with Britain. The French had gained what many of them had wanted for almost a decade, and it had been suggested that this was a key factor in the easy acceptance of Bonaparte's assumption of power for life in August 1802. The Peace of Amiens was greeted with great rejoicing, but only the most naive could have hoped it would last, and, by May 1803, France was again at war. Historians such as Alastair Horne[1] argue that Bonaparte's genius was for war, and that therefore he was bound both to renew the war and to extend his control over France so that he could finance and equip the ever larger armies his strategies demanded. Others suggest that he used the war as the excuse for the extension of power, which was to see him crown himself hereditary emperor in 1804.

Although many historians end their accounts of the Revolution in

1799, or even earlier, it is possible to argue that the Consulate was a key part of the Revolution, in which the preoccupations of the political classes in France remained unchanged, and during which some of the most important gains of the previous ten years were consolidated, so that they were never lost. Irene Collins's pamphlet[2] summarises the views of historians and looks at Bonaparte's whole period in power briefly and clearly.

Certainly many of the problems which had confronted the reformers of 1789, and which had brought about the radicalisation of the Revolution, remained to be solved. The two analyses in this chapter consider whether the position of First Consul was in fact a monarchical one, and the extent to which Bonaparte betrayed the Revolution he had, as an officer, sworn to serve.

ANALYSIS (1): HOW SIMILAR WAS THE POSITION OF THE FIRST CONSUL TO THAT OF A MONARCH OF FRANCE BEFORE 1791?

Bonaparte's seizure of power bore no relationship to the normal and peaceful mechanisms by which French kings took the throne. The Constitution of 1791 merely confirmed generations of tradition in declaring that the monarchy in France was hereditary in the male line. A seizure of power by military force was a very different form of accession, and appears to have come as a surprise even to those who thought they knew Bonaparte well. This meant that Bonaparte lacked the atmosphere of Divine Right which in theory at least, surrounded the anointed king.

Bonaparte's career until 1799 had had its moments of glory, but he did not appear to be politically driven. Born in 1769, educated to be an officer under the *ancien régime*, his promotion chances were much enhanced when he took the oath to the nation in 1791, since those who did not emigrated in large numbers. Chance ensured that it was he who 'saved' Toulon, and, thanks to his old friend Saliceti, he survived the purge which followed Thermidor. Paul Barras became his patron and sponsor, employing him to deal with the Royalist rising of 13 Vendémaire IV. Barras also introduced him to his first wife, Joséphine who, according to Correlli Barnett, was 'shallow, easily bored, and spendthrift',[3] but with whom Bonaparte appears to have fallen passionately in love. Louis XVI had also been burdened with an extravagant and under-educated wife! Bonaparte's triumphs in Italy brought France close to a victorious peace, with only Britain holding out against it. It has been suggested that both the ultimate defeat of Britain and the furthering of General Bonaparte's career pointed towards Egypt. Bonaparte's lines of communication to France were cut by British naval victories, but the last news that the French had was of the triumph of the battle of the Pyramids, which confirmed Bonaparte's hero status. His return to France was therefore untarnished by any suggestion that he had abandoned his army, and his status in France was certainly higher than that of any Dauphin on his accession to the throne. In ruling France, he had the advantage of a Constitution which he had written himself and of which he was to say, in his retirement, 'Constitutions should be short, and obscure'.

Kings before 1791 were said to be absolute but were limited by all kinds of constraints and controls. The Church had an almost autonomous status. Bonaparte ensured that the Church was merely a branch of the civil service. Kings were anointed by the Church, and thus owed their authority to God: Bonaparte took power through his own strength, camouflaged as 'the General Will' which, as Correlli Barnett acidly remarks, 'became synonymous with General Bonaparte'.[4] Indeed, when he became emperor in 1804, he crowned himself, albeit in the presence of the Pope.

The First Consul's choice of ministers was a far more personal one than had been possible for the kings of France. Bonaparte established a system of meeting his ministers individually, in order to give his instructions. In the same way, Bonaparte chose which 'ordinary' citizens he would consult; kings of France had mechanisms for consulting 'the people' but these had fallen into disuse and thus, when the Estates General met in 1789, the effect was revolutionary. Bonaparte's legislative body was, until 1814, submissive and compliant.

Kings of France had controlled local government, with the intendants replacing the traditional power of the provincial nobles. Bonaparte may be said to have restored the system of intendants, but his prefects were far more his own creatures: the Minister of the Interior, Lucien Bonaparte, discussed each appointment with him and again, Bonaparte was not limited to a particular class, but could choose any citizen he wanted. Once the prefects were in place, their links with Paris were close and the rules governing their conduct specific.

As for the policy preoccupations of the kings of France, Bonaparte shared many of them: involvement in possibly unnecessary wars had damaged the economy of *ancien régime* France, and Bonaparte was to pursue the European war with only a brief interlude. The traditional enmity towards Britain, which had persuaded Louis XVI to help the

American colonists, continued to block any rational negotiations; and the claims of France to the Low Countries, a theatre of war from the sixteenth century, were maintained by Bonaparte to the end.

Tax collection was perhaps fairer under Bonaparte than it had been under the kings. There were no exemptions, and assessments were reasonably equitable. The social and regional variations which had so embittered the Third Estate had been removed. Revenue collection was certainly more efficient, since the tax farmers were no more, and corruption was fiercely dealt with. Bonaparte expressed more interest in other aspects of the economy than the King had done, establishing and encouraging technical institutions and ensuring that the education system produced engineers and manufacturers, rather than clerics.

Police control and limitations on personal freedom had been a focus of condemnation by the Philosophes before the Revolution, but had not been entirely efficient: a whole industry of importing and distributing banned texts had flourished in the 1770s and 1780s. Bonaparte's police were more thorough, and so swingeing were the penalties that self-censorship rapidly became the safest path for a newspaper to take. Bonaparte closed down sixty of the seventy-three newspapers in Paris in January 1800, and had a weekly summary prepared of all printed material, but he was soon able to tell his Chief of Police, Fouché, 'They only print what I want them to'. In the same way, the hated *lettres de cachet* appear limited and inefficient when compared to Bonaparte's and Fouché's record of police spies, trials without jury and imprisonment without trial. Bonaparte's brief experience as a Jacobin leader in Ajaccio had taught him how to recognise, and deal with, potential opponents.

The judiciary had stood apart from the kings of the *ancien régime*: while the King was nominally the supreme judge, the training of lawyers and judges had been a matter for the Parlements, with their inherent privileges and mechanisms. The Parlements decided whether the King's laws were acceptable within the fundamental laws of France. Under the Consulate, there were no such constraints on the legislator. The judges were his appointees, and held office entirely at his pleasure; the courts disposed of those who opposed or questioned the government, far more rapidly than had been possible in the reign of Louis XVI. Imprisonment and deportation became regularly used instruments of control under Bonaparte

Kings of France were fathers to their people and had a sense of duty and service. Bonaparte, too, believed that he was essential to the good and glory of France, but was able to make his own decisions about what constituted the good of France in a way which was not open to the king. Finally, while the monarchy of France was hereditary and permanent, and the position of First Consul was supposed to be held for ten years, Bonaparte's strength was demonstrated when he changed his own constitution, first to give him the role for life and then to become a hereditary monarch. All in all, no monarch of the *ancien régime* had anything approaching the power which Bonaparte had been permitted to take for himself.

Questions

1. How significant to Bonaparte's exercise of power was his claim that the people approved his Constitution?
2. How far is it true to say that the Concordat was a key aspect of Bonaparte's control of France?

ANALYSIS (2): DID BONAPARTE BETRAY THE REVOLUTION?

There are as many views on Bonaparte's rise to power as there are historians. D. G. Wright[5] suggests that perceptions of such a strong character must vary according to the individual temperament of the commentator. Marxist historians regard the Coup of Brumaire as a plot supported by the bourgeois merchants to bring them victory in war and a return to profitable trading. On the other hand, Martyn Lyons[6] suggests that French citizens brought the dictatorship on themselves by their apathy and reluctance to take part in local government or to stand for election, thus making the coup extremely simple, and Bonaparte's position instantly secure. If he took and held power with the acquiescence of the French, is it possible to say that he betrayed the Revolution? The evolutionary nature of the Revolution also complicates the issue: which revolution is Bonaparte accused of betraying: the Revolution of 1791, or the Revolution of the Directory?

Some of the gains of the Revolution were certainly reversed or neutralised by Bonaparte. The voting structure, limited though it was to active citizens alone, was reduced to a meaningless ritual, since the legislative body had little power, and the First Consul alone had the right to select members of the Tribunate. Local democracy was replaced by the central appointment of the prefects and mayors. On the other hand, local autonomy had been side-stepped during 1793 and 1794, when the Representatives of the Convention had been sent into the *départements*, so the structure put in place by Bonaparte was not unfamiliar.

The treatment of the Church by the Revolution had been a matter of great controversy. The Constituent Assembly had determined that the Catholic Church should lose its virtual autonomy, and its property. The Terror had ordered the end of the Christian religion, but the attempts to dechristianise had made little impact on the ordinary citizens. Bonaparte recognised how unpopular these changes had been, and an early priority was his negotiation of a new Concordat. The citizens of France were given back, as they saw it, the religion of their forefathers, but the Catholic Church, both liturgically and economically, was closer to the Constitutional Church of 1790 than to the powerful institution it had been before 1789. Bonaparte had ensured that the Church was not, as in the *ancien régime*, a state within a state. He had, perhaps, betrayed the most radical views of the Revolution, but had guaranteed the overall control of the State, while returning the faith of the people and ending the inconvenient and unpopular calendar of the Revolution.

A reason for the Concordat was to strengthen Bonaparte's rule. At the same time he took firm measures against any opponents, whether potential or actual. The army contained many who opposed his religious changes: the slave rebellion in Haiti provided the perfect opportunity to remove such dissidents from France. Of the 25,000 troops sent to deal with it, it is estimated that more than half died of yellow fever. Similarly, when a Royalist bomb plot was uncovered in December 1800, Bonaparte seized the opportunity to blame it on the Jacobins, and many were guillotined, with over a hundred more being exiled or imprisoned. The regime of the Terror had operated in similar ways to remove large numbers of potential or actual opponents. Press censorship and the use of police spies ensured that anti-government opinions were not publicly aired. The Declaration of the Rights of Man had guaranteed freedom of expression; but this freedom had already been eroded before Bonaparte's coup. The Terror had seen both moral and political censorship, and the Directory had on several occasions exercised its constitutional right to censor the press. Bonaparte appears merely to have been more efficient.

Equality had been the most treasured achievement of the Revolution. From August 1789, official distinctions between classes had been removed, and careers opened to all. Distinctions between active and passive citizens had been economic rather class-based, and the enfranchising of soldiers, regardless of their tax-paying abilities, had confirmed that service to the nation could take many forms. At the height of the Terror, even the use of the respectful form in speech had been 'suspect' behaviour, as had standing aside for people in the street. In practice, of course, the assemblies and governments of the

Revolution had, almost without exception, been made up of educated men from prosperous backgrounds, or, like Bonaparte himself, from backgrounds of some privilege. Once in power, Bonaparte made it clear that he was prepared to use men from any background, provided they were loyal and competent. From May 1802, there were even honours and titles to be obtained, though the Legion of Honour was open to all and people from all levels in society might be rewarded. 'Men are ruled by toys', Bonaparte is supposed to have said.

One purpose of the Revolution had been to do away with the enormous financial and economic injustices which marked the *ancien régime*. There had never been an intention to equalise property, however, and the few groups, such as the *Enragés*, who had preached this message had soon been neutralised. Some peasants had gained land, by their own actions, in the summer of 1789, and no attempt was made to remove these lands or to reimpose rents and dues. The weakness of other parts of the economy was worsened by the war and, while Bonaparte prolonged it, he had not begun it. The financial situation had been made worse by the Revolution's prodigal issuing of *assignats*, and temporary draconian attempts to alleviate the problem had failed and had probably been one of the factors leading to the fall of Robespierre in 1794. The Directory, and not Bonaparte, had solved this problem: the ending of the *assignats*, and the liquidation by Ramel, had provided the foundation on which to build a more stable financial structure, which survived until the pressures of prolonged war finally destroyed it. Perhaps the citizens of France would have preferred no taxes at all. But, given the inevitability of taxation, Bonaparte did nothing new, except increase the efficiency and thus the equitable nature of the system.

D. M. G. Sutherland suggests that Bonaparte's main motive was to establish a government above faction, which would be efficient in harnessing all of France to the war effort.[7] Others, notably Correlli Barnett,[8] suggest that personal ambition was a far more significant contributor to his seizure and retention of power. Bonaparte certainly held power without consulting the French people; he took away many of the freedoms they had been guaranteed in 1789; he taxed them more heavily than they had been taxed before. But he did not completely betray the whole Revolution. It was his emasculated legislature (under allied pressure) which eventually made him give up his power; and, after his final removal, it became clear that France would not again accept absolute monarchy; that some kind of elected assembly was to be an essential feature of French government and that social distinctions were to be earned rather than inherited. His regime as Consul had been scarcely more dictatorial than some periods of the Terror and the Directory. He had, admittedly, then moved to monarchy, but it is clear that many of the Constitution writers of the Year III had been thinking along these lines. What Bonaparte did which lays him open to the accusation of betrayal was to hold on to, and to increase, his power, unchecked, for over fifteen years. Other revolutionary regimes which had attempted to do this had been overthrown. Thus, perhaps the worst accusation that can be levelled at his period as First Consul is that he used the war, and the apathy of the French nation, to ensure that he could not be removed.

Questions

1. How far is it true to say that the Coup of Brumaire was entirely due to the weaknesses of the Directory?
2. At what date do you consider that the French Revolution ended?

SOURCES

The first group of sources deals with the mechanisms by which Bonaparte came to power as First Consul and the government which he established. The second group considers Bonaparte's attitudes to government, and to the Revolution.

1. BONAPARTE'S COUP AND HIS GOVERNMENT

Source A: recollections by Barras, writing some years after the event.

The outrage meditated . . . was one very difficult to execute in the very heart of Paris, where all the constitutional authorities had their seat . . . A secret rendezvous was made . . . The principal conspirators [included] Lucien Bonaparte. It was at this satanic gathering that it was settled that the Councils and the Directorate should be transferred unawares to Saint-Cloud . . .

No sooner does the Council of Five Hundred perceive the General with his grenadiers, when it rises in a body by a spontaneous movement. 'Down with the tyrant' vociferate a number of deputies . . . The new Cromwell is hurried away by his grenadiers . . . Lucien tells the soldiery that, as President of the Councils, he orders them to turn out . . . 'the brigands armed with stilettos who call themselves representatives of the people'. . . . The Grenadiers advance with fixed bayonets and the deputies yield to force . . . Alleged legislative councils were appointed to draw up a constitution. Three provisional consuls were to govern until the alleged new social pact should be framed.

Source B: proclamation by Bonaparte, 19 Brumaire VIII.

On my return to Paris I found all authority in chaos and agreement only on the one truth that the Constitution was half destroyed and incapable of preserving liberty . . . The Council of Ancients summoned me; I answered its appeal. A plan for general reform had been drawn up by men upon whom the nation is accustomed to look as the defenders of liberty, equality and property. That plan needed calm examination . . . Accordingly, the Council of Ancients resolved upon the removal of the Legislative Body to Saint-Cloud; it gave me the responsibility of disposing the force necessary for its independence. I believed it my duty to my fellow citizens, to the soldiers perishing in our armies . . . to accept the command. The Councils reassembled at Saint-Cloud . . . assassins created terror within. Several deputies of the Council of Five Hundred, bearing daggers and firearms, uttered threats of death all around them. I presented myself at the Council of Five Hundred alone, unarmed . . . The stilettos which menaced the deputies were instantly raised against their liberator. Cries of 'outlaw' were heard against the defender of the law, the savage cry of the assassins against the force destined to crush them. They pressed around the President, threatening, arms in their hands, ordering him to declare my outlawry. Told of this, I ordered him to be saved from their fury, and six grenadiers rescued him . . . and cleared the Chamber. Intimidated, the seditious dispersed and disappeared. The majority, safe from their threats, returned freely and peacefully to the chamber, heard the proposals made to them for the public good, debated and prepared the salutary resolution which is to become the new and provisional law of the Republic.

Source C: extracts from the Constitution of the Year VIII (13 December 1799).

Art. 39. The government is entrusted to three Consuls, appointed for ten years and indefinitely re-eligible . . . The Constitution appoints Citizen Bonaparte . . . to be First Consul . . .

41. The First Consul promulgates the laws; he appoints and dismisses all the members of the Council of State, the ministers, ambassadors . . . the officers of the armed forces, the members of local administrations and the Government's attorneys before the courts.

42. In the other acts of the Government the Second and Third Consuls have a consultative role . . .

43. The salary of the first Consul will be 500,000 francs during the Year VIII. The salary of each of the other Consuls equals three-tenths of that of the First.

Source D: letter from Bonaparte to the Minister of the Interior, 15 February 1801.

The First Consul is informed, Citizen Minister, that certain prefects believe themselves authorised to interpret the acts of the Government . . . the Consuls desire that prefects be advised . . . that it is their duty to conform literally to orders unless, after making representations to the ministers, they find themselves authorised [to make changes] by precise instructions.

Source E: Bonaparte to Citizen Fouché, Minister of Police, 5 April 1800.

You are to instruct the Prefect of Police to take whatever steps are necessary:
1. To prevent any bill-posting on the walls of Paris, or any crying of papers or pamphlets without a police licence.
2. To prevent the print-dealers displaying for sale anything contrary to sound morals, or to the policy of the government.

Questions

1. Explain what Bonaparte meant by 'on my return' in Source B. [1]
*2. Comment on the powers and privileges allocated to the First Consul (Source C). To what extent does this source indicate that the other two consuls were merely figureheads? [4]
3. Discuss and account for the difference in tone between sources D and E. [5]
4. How far do Sources A and B agree about the events of 18 Brumaire? By what methods do the two writers make clear their own points of view? [7]
5. To what extent do these sources reveal the First Consulate to have been a dictatorship? Is the impression supplied by these sources supported by your own extended knowledge? [8]

Worked answer:

*2. The First Consul was given full powers over the administration of France, since he appointed and dismissed all key officials both civil and military, domestic and foreign; the pretence of a separation of powers as enshrined in the constitution was negated by the fact that the First Consul promulgated all the laws, leaving the legislature merely to pass them. And the judiciary now fell fully under the control of the First Consul. The privileges, other than the salary differential, are not clearly described here. In fact, the uniforms, and living accommodation of the

First Consul marked him out from the other two almost as much as his powers did. Certainly the phrase 'consultative role', and the much smaller salaries authorised to the two other consuls indicate their subordinate role; and the history of the first years of the Consulate confirms that their functions were purely ornamental, while all the power was wielded by the first consul.

2. BONAPARTE'S ATTITUDE TO GOVERNMENT

Source F: extracts from Bonaparte's memoirs, written after 1815.

I was convinced that France could exist only as a monarchy; but, the French people being more desirous of equality than of liberty . . . there was of necessity a complete abolition of the aristocracy. If it was difficult to construct a republic on a solid basis without an aristocracy, the difficulty of establishing a monarchy was much greater. To form a constitution in a country without any kind of aristocracy would be as vain as to attempt to navigate in one element only. The French Revolution undertook a problem as difficult of solution as the direction of a balloon . . . My ideas were fixed . . . The organisation of the Consulate had presented nothing in contradiction of them; it taught unanimity and that was the first step. This point gained, I was quite indifferent as to the forms and denominations of the several constituted bodies; I was a stranger to the Revolution: it was natural that the will of those men who had followed it through all its phases would prevail in questions as difficult as they were abstract.

Source G: extracts from letters and conversations of Bonaparte addressed to his brother Joseph.

Spring 1800. Here every thing goes from good to better. The Prefects are going to their posts and I hope that, in a month, France will at last be an organised state . . . I have composed my Council of State of ex-members of the Constituent Assembly, of moderates, Feuillants, Royalists, Jacobins. I am national: I like honest men of all colours.

Summer 1803. I haven't been able to understand yet what good there is in an opposition. Whatever it may say, its only result is to diminish the prestige of authority in the eyes of the people.

Source H: Napoleon Bonaparte to the Minister of the Interior, Lucien Bonaparte, 25 December 1799.

Since 1790, the 36,000 local bodies have been like 36,000 orphan girls . . . they have been neglected or defrauded for the past ten years by the municipal trustees of the Convention or of the Directory. A new set of mayors ... has generally meant nothing more than a fresh form of robbery ... The prefects and sub-prefects will be warned to bring the whole force of the administration to bear upon the insolvent municipalities and get rid at once of any mayors ... who do not see eye to eye with them as to local improvement.

Source I: reported conversation between Bonaparte and his brother after the signing of the Concordat, 1801.

'We're going to Mass today. What will Paris say about it?'
'The audience will look at the play, and will hiss if it does not please.'
'Then I shall have the Church cleared by the guards!'
'But what if the grenadiers join in the hissing?'
'They won't. My old war dogs will be just as respectful in Notre-Dame as they were in the Cairo mosques. They will keep their eyes on me, and when they see that their general is serious and well behaved, they will follow his example, saying to themselves, "Those are the orders of the day!"'

Source J: from Bonaparte's memoirs, written after 1815.

The Christian religion is the religion of a civilised people and is entirely spiritual ... The Christian religion was three or four centuries in establishing itself, and its progress was slow. It requires much time to destroy, by the mere influence of argument, a religion consecrated by time; and still more when the new religion neither serves nor kindles any passion.

Questions

1. Briefly explain who Bonaparte meant when, in Source G, he referred to Feuillants and Jacobins. [2]
2. By comparing the tone and content of Sources I and J, discuss which of the two is more likely to reflect Bonaparte's real attitude to the Catholic Church. [4]
*3. How far do you agree with Bonaparte's comment in Source F, 'I was a stranger to the Revolution'? [5]
4. In the light of your knowledge of the changes to local government during the Revolution, comment on the accuracy of Bonaparte's description of the local authorities in Source H. [6]
5. Using these sources and your own knowledge, discuss the view that Bonaparte was far more concerned with maintaining his own control over France than with the good of the French nation. [8]

Worked answer

*3. [This question offers an opportunity to demonstrate some knowledge of Bonaparte's earlier career. It is worth discussing the nature of the sources briefly, to establish the reliability of the comment itself.]

Bonaparte's claim to be a 'stranger to the Revolution' was made in his memoirs, written while he was in exile after 1815, and, as part of his rewriting of his own personal history, was intended to distance himself from the actual events of the Brumaire Coup. It is not entirely accurate. As the child of Corsican freedom fighters, Bonaparte had greeted the Revolution with approbation, and had readily taken the oath of allegiance to the nation rather than to the King. He had attempted to turn revolutionary fervour to his own advantage by taking the lead in the Ajaccio Jacobin Club and suggesting ways of bringing the counter-revolutionaries there under control.

Bonaparte was in Paris on 10 August 1792, and was later to remark that, had the King mounted a horse and addressed the crowd, rather than scurrying to the Convention, the monarchy might have survived. He had friends in the Convention, and his heroism at Toulon brought him contacts in the highest circles of the Terror administration, including Maximilian Robespierre's brother Augustin.

When the Constitution of the Year III was published, it was Bonaparte who dispersed the demonstration with his 'whiff of grape-shot', and it is clear that he knew precisely how to deal with hostile rioters. He certainly knew how to address friendly crowds, since his soldiers were the ordinary citizens of France, though of course the content and reception of his stirring speeches are recorded only by himself, rather than by neutral listeners.

On the other hand, Bonaparte had been away from France for much of the period of the Directory, first in Italy and then in Egypt, so his detailed knowledge of the personnel of the councils and of their probable attitudes would be limited. His perceptive – and up to date – metaphor, comparing the progress of France to that of a balloon, indicates that he knew well what had been happening, but preferred to maintain the myth that he was merely obeying the orders of the 'defenders of liberty, equality and property', and that his takeover had been forced upon him.

NOTES AND SOURCES

1. WHY DID THE FRENCH REVOLUTION BEGIN?

1 G. C. Comninel: *Rethinking the French Revolution*, Verso (New York 1987).
2 Georges Lefebvre: *The Coming of the French Revolution* (New York 1957).
3 Karl Marx and Friedrich Engels: *The Communist Manifesto*, Pelican (London ed. 1964).
4 Claude Manceron: *Blood of the Bastille*, Touchstone (New York 1987), p. 309.
5 R. Birn in R. Darnton and D. Roche: *Revolution in Print*, University of California Press, (London 1989), p. 56.
Source A: Controller-General Calonne speaks at the opening of the Assembly of Notables, 22 February 1787.
Source B: the president of the Parlement's speech at the Lit de Justice, 6 August 1787.
Source C: extract from British Embassy despatches.
Source D: memorandum of the Princes of the Blood, 12 December 1788.
Source E: Council of State of the King, 27 December 1788.
Source F: extracts from Arthur Young: *Travels in France*.
Source G: extract from L.S. Mercier: *Tableau de Paris 1783–9*.
Source H: extracts from British Embassy despatches.
Source I: extracts from the first part of *Qu'est-ce que le Tiers Etat*, January 1789.
Source J: letter from Gouverneur Morris to Carmichael, US Chargé d'affaires in Madrid, 25 February 1789.

2. WHEN DID DEVELOPMENTS IN FRANCE BECOME REVOLUTIONARY?

1 Claude Manceron: *Blood of the Bastille*, Touchstone, (New York 1987), p. 444.
2 Jeremy D. Popkin in R. Darnton and D. Roche: *Revolution in Print*, (London 1989), p. 150.
3 H. C. Barnard: *Education in the French Revolution*, Cambridge University Press (Cambridge 1969).
4 Antoine de Baecque in R. Darnton and D. Roche: *Revolution in Print*, University of California Press, (London 1989) p. 165.
5 D. G. Sutherland: *France 1789–1815: Revolution and Counter Revolution*, Fontana (London 1985).
6 Alan Forrest: *The French Revolution and the Poor*, Blackwell (Oxford 1981).
Source A: extract from the Diary of Gouverneur Morris.
Source B: 20 June letter from Necker to the Lieutenant of the Paris police.
Source C: Lavaux, a laywer, writing much later, about a visit to the Cordelier district on 13 July.
Source D: from 'Les Révolutions de Paris', no.1, 17 July 1789.
Source E: Camille Desmoulins: *Discours de la lanterne aux Parisiens*, September 1789.
Source F: *The Times* 12 October 1789.
Source G: preliminary *cahier* of the parish of Boisse.
Source H: Arthur Young at Strasbourg, 20 July 1789.
Source I: a complaint to the National Assembly by the Comte de Germiny, 20 August 1789.
Source J: Antoine, Comte de Rivarol, writing in *Le Journal Politique National*, 1790.
Source K: account by Drouet, postmaster at Sainte-Menehould, a few miles from Varennes.

3. THE CONSTITUENT ASSEMBLY

1 Simon Schama: *Citizens*, Penguin (London 1989).
2 Michael P. Fitzsimmons: *The Remaking of France* Cambridge University Press (Cambridge 1994).
3 Daniel Arasse: *The Guillotine and the Terror*, Allen Lane (London 1989), p. 165.
4 Arasse: *The Guillotine and the Terror*, pp. 123–4.
5 Florin Aftalion. *The French Revolution: An Economic Interpretation* Cambridge University Press (Cambridge 1990), p. 89.
6 Aftalion: *The French Revolution*, p. 93.

7 Colin Jones, ed.: *Longmans Companion to the French Revolution* (London 1988) p. 237.

8 Andrew Freeman: *The Compromising of Louis XVI*, Exeter Studies in History (Exeter 1989).

Source A: the ending of feudal dues, 4 August 1789.

Source B: extracts from the Declaration of the Rights of Man and of the Citizen, 26 August 1789.

Source C: Bill proposed by Dr Guillotin, for the reform of the penal system, January 1790.

Source D: extracts from the Civil Constitution of the Clergy, 12 July 1790.

Source E: petition from Claude Louis Rousseau, a clergyman who had been a preacher at court, 30 May 1790. One of the documents from the *armoire de fer*.

Source F: from the Diary of the Bailly, 17 July 1789.

Source G: Louis' Declaration of 20 June 1791.

Source H: the Declaration of Pilnitz, 27 August 1791.

Source I: extracts from the Constitution, 14 September 1791.

Source J: memorandum, read to the royal council by Narbonne, 24 February 1792, preserved in the *armoire de fer*.

4. THE WAR IN EUROPE

1 T. C. W. Blanning: *The Origins of the French Revolutionary Wars*, Macmillan (London 1986).

2 Florin Aftalion: *The French Revolution: An Economic Interpretation*, Cambridge University Press (Cambridge 1990).

3 J. Godechot: *France and the Atlantic Revolution*, Fontana (London 1978).

4 Simon Schama: *Citizens*, Penguin (London 1989), p. 567.

5 Norman Hampson: *Danton*, Duckworth (London 1978).

6 Hampson: *Danton*, p. 82.

7 G. Lenôtre: *The September Massacres*, Hutchinson (London 1929).

8 Colin Jones, ed.: *Longmans Companion to the French Revolution* (London 1988), p. 237.

9 Thomas Carlyle: *The French Revolution* (London 1837).

Source A: anonymous and undated memorandum from the *armoire de fer* headed: 'Observations on the speech proposed to the King' (by which he was to accept the constitution, i.e. September 1791).

Source B: speech in the Assembly by Pierre Vergniaud, 27 December 1791.

Source C: speech by Robespierre at the Jacobin Club, 11 January 1792.

Source D: declaration of war on Austria, 29 April 1792.
Source E: a letter from Chauvelin to Lebrun, 28 August 1792.
Source F: a part of the Brunswick Manifesto, 25 July 1792.
Source G: proclamation, probably drafted by Danton, 25 August 1792.
Source H: extracts from a speech by Danton, 28 August 1792.
Source I: *The Times*, 8 September 1792, but relating to several days earlier.
Source J: two extracts from the debate on the sentence of the King, January 1793.

5. THE TERROR

1 R. R. Palmer: *Twelve Who Ruled* (Princeton 1941).
2 Alan Forrest: *The French Revolution and the Poor*, Blackwell (Oxford 1981).
3 Florin Aftalion: *The French Revolution: An Economic Interpretation*, Cambridge University Press (Cambridge 1990), pp. 134–6.
4 D. G. Sutherland: *France 1789–1815 Revolution and Counter Revolution*, Fontana (London 1985), p. 235.
5 Duncan Townson: *France in Revolution*, Hodder and Stoughton (London 1990), pp. 93–4.
6 Josh Brooman: *Carrier and the drownings at Nantes*, Longmans (London 1987).
7 Forrest: *The French Revolution and the Poor*, pp. 143–4.
8 Aftalion: *The French Revolution*, p. 160.
9 Townson: *France in Revolution*, pp. 93–4.
Source A: extracts from the decree of the General Maximum, 29 September 1793.
Source B: extracts from a speech by Saint-Just in the Convention, 19 Vendémiaire II (10 October 1793).
Source C: report from *The Times*, 20 November 1793.
Source D: from a report by the American Ambassador, Gouverneur Morris, 18 April 1794.
Source E: extract from the Decree of 18 Floréal II, recognising the Supreme Being (7 May 1794).
Source F: extracts from a speech by Robespierre at the Jacobin Club, 1 Frimaire II (21 November 1793).
Source G: extracts from a police report, Paris, 18 Nivose II (January 1794).
Source H: part of a speech by Collot d'Herbois at the Jacobin Club, Ventose II.
Source I: from Robespierre's speech to the Convention, 12 Germinal II (31 March 1794).
Source J: some statistics about the number of death sentences.

6. THE DIRECTORY AND ITS ACHIEVEMENTS

1 Martin Lyons: *France Under the Directory*, Cambridge University Press (Cambridge 1975).
2 Duncan Townson: *France in Revolution* (London 1990), pp. 115,117.
3 W. Doyle: *The Oxford History of the French Revolution*, Oxford University Press (Oxford 1989), p. 332.
4 D. M. G. Sutherland: *France 1789–1815 Revolution and Counter Revolution* p. 333.
5 Doyle: *The Oxford History of the French Revolution*, p. 355.
6 Sutherland: *France 1789–1815*, p. 335.
7 Townson: *France in Revolution*, p. 117.
8 Florin Aftalion: *The French Revolution*, p. 178.
9 Alan Forrest: *The French Revolution and the Poor* pp. 160–1.
Source A: report by Barère, 28 July 1794.
Source B: François Antoine Boissy d'Anglas in *Le Moniteur*, 1795.
Source C: Nicolas Ruault, journalist, describes the hardship of the winter 1794–5.
Source D: letter from Napoleon Bonaparte to his brother, autumn 1795.
Source E: manifesto of the Directors, 5 November 1795.
Source F: the Doctrine of Babeuf, May 1796.
Source G: the Manifesto of the Equals, May 1796, Gracchus Babeuf.
Source H: a comment by Bonaparte, during his exile.
Source I: 'Each to his own bankruptcy', cartoon from September 1797.
Source J: report to the Directors by a Commissioner in Seine et Oise, 1700.

7. THE COUNTER-REVOLUTION

1 Colin Jones, ed.: *Longmans Companion to the French Revolution* (London 1988), p. 199.
2 Jones: *Longmans Companion to the French Revolution*, p. 119.
3 W. Doyle: *The Oxford History of the French Revolution* p. 327.
4 Doyle: *The Oxford History of the French Revolution*, p. 316.
5 P. M. Jones: *The Peasantry in the French Revolution* (Cambridge 1988), p. 234.
6 J. Godechot: *The Counter Revolution: Doctrine and Action* (Princeton 1971).
7 Niall Ferguson: *Virtual History*, Picador (London 1997).
8 Doyle: *The Oxford History of the French Revolution*, p. 117.
9 Godechot: *The Counter Revolution*.

10 Doyle: *The Oxford History of the French Revolution*.
Source A: letter from the Count of Provence to his brother the Count of Artois, 28 January 1793.
Source B: 'Address to the French' written by Abbé Bernier, May 1793.
Source C: extract from Joseph Farington's Diary, 21 July 1793.
Source D: a peasant's contemporary account of the warfare in the Vendée.
Source E: memoirs of Mme la Marquise de Rochejacquelin, published in 1817.
Source F: Brissot in the Legislative Assembly, 1791.
Source G: Collot d'Herbois to Duplay in Paris, from Commune Affranchie (Lyon) 15 Frimaire II (5 December 1793).
Source H: from the memoirs of General Turreau, published in 1824.
Source I: proclamation of the Catholic and Royal Army of Brittany to the inhabitants of La Prevalaye, 21 April 1795.
Source J: letter from Charette about the Treaty of Mabilais, May 1795.

8. DID THE FRENCH REVOLUTION END WITH BONAPARTE?

1 A. Horne: *Napoleon, Master of Europe*, Macmillan (London 1979).
2 Irene Collins: *Napoleon*, Historical Association (London 1986).
3 Correlli Barnett: *Bonaparte*, Allen and Unwin (London 1978), p. 40.
4 Barnett: *Bonaparte*, p. 70.
5 D. G. Wright: *Napoleon and Europe*, Longmans Seminar Studies (London 1984).
6 Martin Lyons: *France under the Directory* (Cambridge 1975).
7 D. M. G. Sutherland: *France 1789–1815, Revolution and Counter Revolution* (London 1985), pp. 336–8.
8 Barnett: *Bonaparte*.
Source A: recollections by Barras, writing some years after the event.
Source B: proclamation by Bonaparte, 19 Brumaire VII.
Source C: extracts from the Constitution or the Year VIII (13 December 1799).
Source D: letter from Bonaparte to the Minister of the Interior, 15 February 1801.
Source E: Bonaparte to Citizen Fouché, Minister of Police, 5 April 1800.
Source F: extracts from Bonaparte's memoirs, written after 1815.
Source G: extracts from letters and conversations of Bonaparte addressed to his brother Joseph.
Source H: Napoleon Bonaparte to the Minister of the Interior, Lucien Bonaparte, 25 December 1799.

Source I: reported conversation between Bonaparte and his brother after the signing of the Concordat, 1801.
Source J: from Bonaparte's memoirs, written after 1815.

SELECT BIBLIOGRAPHY

PRIMARY SOURCES

There are many collections of primary sources about the French Revolution. Some of these are: J. J. Thompson: *The French Revolution: Documents* (Oxford 1933); J. M. Roberts and J. Hardman: *The French Revolution* (documents), two volumes (Oxford 1966); John Hardman, *The French Revolution 1785–1795* (London 1981); R. Cobb and C. Jones: *The French Revolution 1789–1795* (London 1989); Leonard W. Cowie: *The French Revolution, Documents and Debates* (London 1987); D. G. Wright: *Revolution and Terror in France* (London 1974). For contemporary accounts of France both before and in the first years of the Revolution, two books are particularly accessible and interesting: Constantia Maxwell, ed.: *Arthur Young's Travels in France* (Cambridge 1929) and B. C. Davenport, ed.: *Gouverneur Morris: A Diary of the French Revolution* (London 1939) A range of the documents found in the *armoire de fer* is printed in Andrew Freeman: *The Compromising of Louis XVI: The Armoire de Fer and the French Revolution* (Exeter 1989).

SECONDARY SOURCES

So much has been written about the French Revolution that this list is of necessity selective. For specific details, statistics and a clear summary, Colin Jones: *The Longman Companion to the French Revolution* (London 1988) is very useful, as is the *Chronicle of the French Revolution* (London 1989) as much for its fascinating illustrations as for its text. Of the many general works about the Revolution, among the most readable and useful are: D. M. G. Sutherland: *France 1789–1815 Revolution and Counter Revolution* (London 1985) and W. Doyle: *The Oxford History of the French Revolution* (Oxford 1989). T. C. W. Blanning: *The French Revolution – Class War or Culture Clash?* (London 1997) and Duncan Townson: *France in Revolution* (London 1990) also provide clear overall summaries. Specific interpretations can be found in J. F. Bosher: *The French Revolution* (London 1990) P. Jones, ed.: *The French Revolution in Social and Political Perspective* (London 1996) and George C. Comninel: *Rethinking the French Revolution: Marxism and the Revisionist Challenge* (London 1987). The economic aspect is fascinatingly discussed in Florin Aftalion: *The French Revolution: An Economic Interpretation* (trans. M. Thom, Cambridge 1990). Simon Schama: *Citizens* (London 1989) contains a wealth of detail in a most readable form.

Particular people, aspects and periods are considered in: J. Hardman: *Louis XVI* (New Haven and London 1993); Dunlop: *Marie Antoinette* (London 1993); Claude Manceron: *Blood of the Bastille* (vol 5 of his account of the Revolution) (London 1989); M. P. Fitzsimmons: *The Remaking of France: The National Assembly and the Constitution of 1791* (Cambridge 1994); Norman Hampson: *The Terror in the French Revolution*, HA Pamphlet General Series 103 (London 1981); Daniel Arasse: *The Guillotine and the Terror* (London 1989); Norman Hampson: *The Life and Opinions of Maximilien Robespierre* (London 1974); Norman Hampson: *Danton* (London 1989); R. Darnton and D. Roche, ed.: *Revolution in Print* (London 1989); H. C. Barnard: *Education in the French Revolution* (Cambridge 1969); P. M. Jones: *The Peasantry in the French Revolution* (Cambridge 1988); Alan Forrest: *The French Revolution and the Poor* (Oxford 1981); Martin Lyons: *France Under the Directory* (Cambridge 1975); J. Godechot: *The Counter Revolution: Doctrine and Action.* (Princeton 1971); D. G. Wright: *Napoleon and Europe* (London 1987); Correlli Barnett: *Bonaparte* (London 1971); Martyn Lyons: *Napoleon Bonaparte and the Legacy of the French Revolution* (London 1994); Geoffrey Ellis: *Napoleon* (London 1997).

INDEX